THE KING'S GOVERNMENT AND THE
COMMON LAW
1471–1641

THE
KING'S GOVERNMENT
AND
THE COMMON LAW
1471 – 1641

By

Sir CHARLES OGILVIE, C.S.I., C.B.E., M.A.

Sometime Lecturer in History in the University of St. Andrews

BASIL BLACKWELL
OXFORD
1958

© BASIL BLACKWELL
OXFORD
1958

Printed by Messrs. Billing and Sons Ltd.,
London Printing Works, Guildford, Surrey,
and bound at the Kemp Hall Bindery
in the city of Oxford.

To
G.E.M.O.
and
M.B.S.B.

ACKNOWLEDGEMENTS

MY attention was first drawn to the influence of the theory and practice of the Common Law on the history of England by the inspiring lectures of Dr. K. W. M. Pickthorn, M.P., of Corpus Christi College, Cambridge, especially those dealing with the Judicial and Parliamentary career of Sir Edward Coke. I also owe much to the advice and criticism of Professor W. L. Burn, of the University of Durham, on the arrangement of the book, on the expansion of certain parts of it, notably those dealing with the Chancery, and on the elimination of irrelevancies.

Any mistakes, on the other hand, either in matters of fact, or in deduction therefrom, are entirely my own work.

C. MACL. G. OGILVIE.

CONTENTS

CHAPTER   PAGE

I. Introductory   1

II. The Origins of the Common Law   9

III. The Development of Common Law Procedure   15

IV. The Disappearance of Equity   25

V. The Creation and Development of the Equitable
Jurisdiction of Chancery till the End of the Fifteenth
Century   34

VI. The Criminal Law   43

VII. The Restoration of Order (I)—The Yorkists   48

VIII. The Restoration of Order (II)—Henry VII   55

IX. The Restoration of Order (III)—Wolsey   67

X. Henry VIII and the Cessation of Projects of Law
Reform   73

XI. The Organization of the Common Law Courts and
Chancery during the Later Tudor and Stuart Periods   79

XII. The Court of Requests from the Reign of Henry VIII   88

XIII. The Court of Chancery in the XVIth and XVIIth
Centuries   91

XIV. The Criminal Jurisdiction of the King's Council from
1540   98

XV. The King's Council and the Civil Law   113

XVI. The Common Lawyer's Counter Attack on Chancery
and the Prerogative Courts   118

XVII. The Direct Attack on the King's Government   134

XVIII. The King's Counter Attack on the Common Law,
and its Defeat   144

XIX. Conclusion   161

Index   169

CHAPTER I

INTRODUCTORY

MUCH has been written about the King's Government in Tudor and Stuart times, and something about that of the Yorkists. One main aspect of the problem facing the "New Monarchy" has however attracted little systematic attention from political and constitutional historians.

There has been no general recognition of the part played by the procedure and practice of the Courts of Justice in the day-to-day administration of the law. It may indeed be said that there has been a failure to perceive the close and organic connection between the social, economic, and political malaise of the fifteenth, sixteenth, and seventeenth centuries, and the hoary but sinewy deformities of the English legal system. It is, moreover, arguable that the struggle of the "New Monarchy" to restore and maintain order was more with the law than with the law breakers. Also it may reasonably be held that the efforts of the King's Government to mitigate the rigours of the Civil Courts in the interests of the ordinary citizen were, in part at least, responsible for the downfall of Charles I.

The main cause for the neglect of this factor may perhaps be found in the undifferentiated use of the word 'law'. The term normally evokes general notions of order, rectitude, and impartial justice, or the idea of a regulating principle, but not detailed considerations of legal technicalities and intricate procedural rules. But they too are 'law'. In England their transcendant import could hardly have been exaggerated up to the second half of the nineteenth century. But as Sir Frederick Pollock wrote (with reference to the practical application of legal principles)—"We have come in this country to look upon law as a subject so technical and difficult, not to say repulsive, that nobody but lawyers can well meddle with it." Maitland held the same opinion. "With all their love of politics and public affairs Englishmen are easily content with knowing nothing of the ordinary Civil law under which they live."[1]

[1] F. Pollock, *Essays in Jurisprudence and Ethics*, London 1882, p. 198, and F. W. Maitland, *Collected Papers*, Vol. II, Cambridge 1911, pp. 162-3.

On the other hand in no country is there, or was there, deeper traditional reverence for the idea of the law than in England. It was held to define, and almost to sanctify, the indefeasible rights of individual freemen, and particularly their rights in property. "As one looks at the Common Law as a whole, one must continually notice the insistent testimony it bears to its feudal origins."[1] There are certainly some pre-Conquest elements to be considered, but these were not altogether alien to the feudal custom of the Anglo-Norman King's tenants-in-chief, which became not only the private law of all free Englishmen, but also the enduring foundation of public law.

It was based upon the fundamental notion of Fealty,[2] not on ultimate obedience to authority, and long after feudalism had decayed, it was almost universally accepted by the politically valid class that the safeguarding of the national liberties depended upon the preservation of what had become a national heritage.

The position of the unique English legal system was also fortified by generally accepted theory. The jurists and political philosophers of the Middle Age held that the positive law of any society acquired its sanction from the Divine Law by which the whole Universe is governed, and this came to be considered to apply to procedural as well as to substantive law. There could be no legislation, at least theoretically, in the modern sense of the word. Law was not made. It was recognized as the result of generations of experience, and then duly declared and accepted. Good law must be old law. The longer positive law had continued unaltered, the more certainly could it be considered to be part of the Divine Law, and the champions of the Common Law in the sixteenth and seventeenth centuries claimed for it an immemorial antiquity. To them it was not a piecemeal system slowly developed from the Royal Writs of the twelfth and thirteenth centuries, but the time-honoured custom of the freemen of England, which had survived not merely the Norman, but the

[1] W. T. Barbour, *History of Contract in Early English Equity*, Oxford, Clarendon Press, 1914, Cap. I, p. 11.

[2] "From the eleventh century at latest the fealty of the subject was compared, and even identified with the homage of the vassal. Although this did not mean that the relationship between monarch and subject was wholly feudalized, in the law of the land the mutual relations of the two were assimilated to the contract between Lord and Vassal." Kern—*Kingship and Law*, Oxford, Blackwell, 1948, p. 121. "All well founded private rights were protected from arbitrary change, as parts of the same objective legal structure as that to which the monarch owed his own authority." Ibid., p. 70.

Saxon conquest, and the main duty of the King was to protect and preserve it. It seems that the "course of the courts" with all its archaic formalism and technical elaboration came to share in the sanctity of the underlying principles. Because the Common Law partook of the nature of the eternally, universally, and immutably binding ordinances of God, and was indeed a reflection of them, or of part of them, it was to be observed by Princes as much as by subjects. This fitted in well with the fundamental notion of Fealty. The law in this sense was sovereign. In spite of the revolution in thought brought about by the Renaissance, and by the doctrine of royal absolutism plausibly extractable from the study of Roman Jurisprudence, the pre-eminent position of the law survived in England till 1641. This may well have been due to the fact that the common or national law had been rooted in feudal custom for four hundred years. The reciprocal character of fealty, and the protection it gave to acknowledged individual rights, ran completely counter to any form of absolutist doctrine.

It cannot be too strongly insisted that the Common Law was public law as well as private. It was regarded as a barrier against arbitrary exactions, which the Roman Law, as received in France, clearly did not provide. As Fortescue said, the King of England was unable "to burden an unwilling people with strange imposts, so that, ruled by laws they themselves desire, they freely enjoy their properties, and are despoiled neither by their own King, nor any other".[1]

The actual exercise of the royal authority was consequently severely restricted. The King's prerogative was to govern. No one in this period would seriously have disputed this, at least until the seventeenth century. The desire of the ancient territorial aristocracy to co-operate with the King, or even to control him, in the business of government had ceased to be effective after Edward IV regained his throne. The newer and potentially more formidable aristocracy of the upper middle class did not begin to show its teeth for nearly a century after 1471. But the exercise of the King's absolute prerogative was in practice limited by the prerogative of the subject, which, save in immediate national emergencies, was equally indefeasible. The King was expected "to live of his own", and to bear not only the expenses of his household, but the cost of carrying

---

[1] Sir John Fortescue, *De Laudibus legum Angliae*, ed. S. B. Chrimes, Cambridge Studies in Legal History, 1942, Cap. IX, p. 25.

on the government of a national kingdom on a largely feudal income
—the rents of his estates and feudal dues, plus customs duties (which
seem to have a purely prerogatival origin) and the largely usurped
profits of justice. Down to the end of the period it was expected that
normally there should be no taxation. Taxation meant to those
interested—the more or less well-to-do—simply war taxation, and
even in times of grave national emergency was granted grudgingly
and insufficiently. "To the King belongs authority over all men, to
the subject property."[1] This dichotomy lies at the root of the difficulties and troubles which constantly beset the Crown, and of the
hampering financial restrictions which were apt to stifle projects of
reform or improvement as well as arbitrary and unpopular measures.
The physical force at the disposal of the King was puny. He had
no standing army, no police, no large paid bureaucracy, because he
could not afford them.

When the English gentry had had some experience of a government which, being backed by military force, did not suffer from
the ancient restraints, a remarkable pamphlet, entitled "A Plea for
limited monarchy, as it was established in this nation before the late
War"[2] was addressed to General Monk. The author, who was perhaps Sir Roger L'Estrange, set out to show that true English liberty
could be supported only by the old English monarchy. The essential nature of the English polity, as it stood before the Great Rebellion, could hardly have been more ably and concisely stated. The
author pointed out that the royal prerogative of government was
absolute only in name, as the King had not the means successfully
to embark on policies disapproved by his subjects. His revenues were
adequate for the upkeep of his court and dignity and (supposedly)
for peacetime government, but wholly insufficient either for military adventure or for domestic tyranny. He could never "presume
to maintain redcoats in time of peace". On the other hand the subject's prerogative was normally maintainable. "Liberty was no less
sacred than majesty; noli me tangere was likewise its motto, and,
in case of any the least infringement, it was resented as if the nation
had received a box on the ear."

What was meant by "the nation", and what by "liberty"? If
"the nation" had meant what it means today, one might conclude
that the bulk of the inhabitants of England would have been highly

[1] Seneca, De Beneficiis.
[2] Harleian Miscellany, ed. Oldys, 1808, Vol. I, pp. 15–18.

content. But it did not. The word meant merely the classes whose opinions the King had at all times to take into account—the nobility, and country gentry, together with the leading townsmen—prosperous merchants, and lawyers. Some thirty or forty thousand only were included.[1] They were, generally speaking, a remarkably closely knit body, or rather, perhaps, a federation of more or less independent but related groups, with one common basic interest. The country gentry, by no means a static but a constantly growing class, regularly recruiting from the ranks of finance, commerce, and the law, after the dissolution of the monasteries and the great accession of wealth and influence which thereby accrued to them, rapidly became the potentially most formidable antagonist of the Crown. They were, in the main, wrapped up in their local interests, and even when they could see beyond them, strongly disliked interference in their doings, economic and other, by the Central Government. They had close and enduring connections, often family ties, with the superior merchants, and also with the upper strata of the legal profession, and the majority were animated by the same constant motive—the protection of their property, and the defeat of measures likely to hamper its increase.

It is hardly too much to say that these classes had for long regarded the maintenance of the "subject's prerogative" as the chief function of law and government. Lockeian doctrines are traceable very far back in English politico-economic thought. Their influence is apparent in L'Estrange's pamphlet, and the main practical argument put forward by other seventeenth-century royalists for the superiority of monarchy to other forms of government was that—at least in England—it gave the best guarantee of the inviolability of subject right. A notable example is supplied by Sir Roger Twysden, a political thinker of considerable learning and insight, who had been a member of the Long Parliament. "The world," he wrote, "now above 5,500 years old, hath found means to limit kings, but never yet any republic. For taxes, as impositions, excise, and such like, who showed princes in Europe that way of raising money but republics?"[2] Some years later a pamphleteer, writing this time in the Whiggish interest, went so far as to state that any invasion of

[1] Thomas Wilson, *The State of England, A.D. 1600*, Camden Miscellany, Vol. XVI, 1936, pp. 19–23.
[2] Sir Roger Twysden, *Certaine considerations upon the government of England*, ed. J. M. Kemble, Camden Society, 1849, p. 10.

private property by the monarch would destroy his title to the throne, and dissolve the constitution.[1]

What was meant by "liberty"? The word has different connotations at different times and among different peoples. Here it seems clearly to mean primarily freedom to possess and acquire, and was fully attainable only by "the nation".

It is therefore not surprising that the Common Law, which was essentially a law of property, and especially of landed property, was regarded by the politically influential class, the backbone of which were the country gentry, as its shield and buckler. Its root principle had become the "Ancient Fundamental Law" of the High Court of Parliament, the bulwark of "the nation" against encroachments by the executive goverment. It was this which was responsible for the adulation with which, for centuries, the Common Law was generally regarded. Even now, in its twilight, there still remains an afterglow.

But at first sight it seems incredible that the methods applied to the decision of cases in the ordinary courts of justice could have endured for nearly six hundred years. Their origins and development will be dealt with moderately fully in the succeeding chapters. Here it is sufficient to say that they were of extreme artificiality, rigidity, and formalism, complicated also by the highest degree of technical refinement, verbal subtlety, and specialized scholarship. These characteristics did undoubtedly give an overwhelming advantage to those who could afford to last the course, and also to pay for the assistance of the most skilled practitioners. Though the law of the King's Court, originally applicable to the merest handful, had become the law of all free men, an ordinary small freeholder could hardly hope to contend with a substantial landowner. The 'Course of the Courts', though not continually abused, except in the fifteenth century, did always give the well-to-do a sense of security against possible litigiousness by their poorer neighbours. It was a not ineffective guarantee of the stability of an ordered society. This seems to have been the principal reason for the strange vitality of the 'ungodly jumble' of the Common Law.[2]

[1] The Original and Design of Magistracy, 1688. *Harleian Miscellany*, ed. Oldys, 1808, Vol. I, p. 5. Cf. also Sir Thomas More, *History of Richard III*, "The gathering of money is the only thing that withdraweth the hearts of Englishmen from their Prince."

[2] "The more elaborate the land law became, and the more subtly it contrived to entangle both present and future generations in the maze of real property law, the more impossible it became for the landed classes to contemplate any interference with the system which assured to them and their children the complicated benefits of inheritance." *Concise History of the Common Law*, T. F. T. Plucknett, London 1948, p. 44.

The Kings themselves, moreover, fully realized the advantage given them by the manifold intricacies of legal procedure, and, *faute de mieux*, were constantly compelled to employ the most skilled and experienced lawyers both to secure their rightful dues, and also to enhance their slender resources by the use not only of legal procedure, but at times of legal chicanery also. The King was the greatest of all litigants, and the best served. He was also by no means always scrupulous. But he was King of all his people, and not merely of 'the nation'. Apart from the prime necessity of repairing the complete breadown of the jury system in both civil and criminal proceedings during the fifteenth century, and the restoration of a reasonable degree of order, something had to be done to check the swelling discontent of the growing lower middle class, and also of the poorer gentry, who found justice effectually denied to them by the intricate maze of technicalities, so infinitely patient of delay and subterfuge, and hence so infinitely costly, which was presented by the civil side of the Common Law. The King was faced therefore by a deeply entrenched and fortified vested interest, in which he too had his part, and by a widespread and increasing volume of grievance against it. It was inevitable in the circumstances of the time that nothing better than palliatives could be found. Radical reform was politically impossible, and was never seriously considered, except, perhaps, by Wolsey. The protracted failure to introduce comparatively simple and certainly obvious measures of procedural reform in the existing courts was doubtless due both to the innate conservatism of the lawyers, and to the easily aroused suspicion and jealousy of their allies in the upper classes. Another subsidiary reason may be found not only in the exalted position of the judges, but also in the respect with which they were universally regarded. They were hardly ever directly mercenary. In an age when the most barefaced corruption was rampant in high places as well as in low, they were almost always strictly honest according to the standards of the time. Apart from the scandals of Edward I's reign, the case of Chief Justice Thorpe in that of Edward III, a few rather dubious instances in the hurly-burly of the fifteenth century, and the open rapacity of Chief Baron Mansfield at the end of the sixteenth,[1] the record of the English judiciary is remarkably unblemished. Bacon, though condemned and admitting the justice of his condemnation, was guilty of no more than following the traditional practice of accepting fees

[1] *Acts of the Privy Council 1590/1.*

and presents. There is no evidence that he allowed them to sway his judgment. It seems certain that there was from early times a high and closely guarded standard of professional honour, fostered presumably in the Inns of Court. The measureless abuse to which the law and lawyers were subjected by dissidents during this period (and before, and after it) was never aimed at the personal reputation of the judges. It is therefore possible, as John Cook, himself a lawyer and a judge, wrote in 1655, that the acknowledged rectitude of the judiciary was a factor in preserving for so long inviolate "the old Circularity and Dilatory Declinationary Pleas and Exceptions, and all those unnecessary delays, which, like Pricking Bryers and Brambles, grew about the Vine of Justice".[1] More than two hundred years later, after the introduction of the reforms most craved by Cook, Sir Frederick Pollock could still write "The merits of our legal system, or rather of those who administer it, do much to hide its defects; the excellence of the workmen prevents us from seeing how faulty the tools are."[2]

Before proceeding to examine the efforts of the King's Government to make the legal system workable, and adaptable to the needs of the majority in changing social conditions (not by reform, but by partial substitution) it is necessary to attempt a brief description of the origin and development of the Common Law. Without some knowledge of this, the principles and practice guiding the day-to-day administration of justice are not intelligible. "Of all the schisms which rend the woven garment of historical understanding, the worst is that which fixes a deep gulf between mediaeval and modern history."[3] This statement is especially true of the history of English law. On one side of its pedigree the Common Law is the direct descendant of the feudal land law of the twelfth and thirteenth centuries, and on the other of mediaeval scholastic education.

[1] Letter from John Cook, the regicide, to the Lord Deputy of Ireland, 6 Aug. 1655. printed in Appendix O to *Irish Life in the 17th century*, by Edward MacLysaght. 1950,
[2] F. Pollock, *Essays in Jurisprudence and Ethics*, London 1882, p. 64.
[3] A. F. Pollard, *Wolsey*, 1929, p. 8.

CHAPTER II

THE ORIGINS OF THE COMMON LAW

IT IS, however, true that certain elements of the English Legal System had descended from the Anglo-Saxon past, though they were not incompatible with Norman notions, but rather the reverse. Indeed, the very essence of what became the Common Law—the absolute right of the freeman to his property, whatever the demands, or needs, of the King might be—may well have been a feature of the local and customary laws of pre-Conquest England.

Secondly the position of the King as the fountain of justice may be equally ancient. From Saxon times, the King had sworn to do justice, equitable justice—to all men. If a complaint of injustice or of failure to obtain a fair hearing were made to him, he was bound by the terms of his coronation oath to intervene.[1] He might either send an order to the court concerned to do or to expedite justice; or he might transfer the case to his own court. So far as is known, the justice administered there must always have been roughly equitable; that is to say, the facts of each individual case were considered on their merits without reference to precedent, and the proceedings were unhampered by technicalities or formalism.

Thirdly there was nothing new about the rigid adherence to the letter of the law, which was characteristic of the developed legal system. The old law law apart from its dependence on the judgment of God, as exemplified in the ordeals, was pre-eminently a law of formal procedure, in which complete verbal accuracy was essential. It may be that the making of a slip, or the mis-spelling of a word or name, was anciently regarded as having been brought about by supernatural agency, as a sign that the claim was false. No attempt was made to ascertain the probability of statements by the detailed examination of witnesses. These features remained recognizable throughout our period, and beyond it. It may be said that they represent survivals from the comparatively remote past which had been

---

[1] Percy Schramm, *A History of the English Coronation*, Oxford 1937; and H. G. Richardson, the English Coronation Oath, *Royal Historical Society's Transactions 1941.*

carried over into the scientifically complex structure of what came to be known as the Common Law.

Fourthly it seems that at least the idea of the jury was known in England some seventy years before the Norman Conquest. The jury, "the Palladium of English liberties", "the bulwark of the British Constitution" is, said Maitland, "French and Royal, not English and popular".[1] There is no doubt that the Conqueror very greatly extended its use, and that under his successors it became an integral part of the English legal system, both on the civil and on the criminal sides. But as Professor Stenton has pointed out, the Wantage Code of Aethelred II provided for the presentation of suspects by a jury composed of the twelve leading thegns of the wapentake concerned, who had to swear that they would neither accuse the innocent, nor shield the guilty. "The Anglo-Norman jury may well have owed as much to English practice as to Carolingian reminiscence."[2] At any rate it was not a completely foreign importation.

There were no other ancient elements except the survival of compurgation or 'oath helping' as a possible defence in certain classes of case. The substantive Common Law was in the main the child of prerogative. Its ascertainable content was based upon the commands, or writs, of the Angevin and Plantagenet Kings, with subsequent additions by way of statute. These writs, whereby the King either directed the doing of justice by the court concerned, or transferred it to the Curia Regis for trial by himself and his council, were at first not at all numerous. The judicial competence of the King's Court, like that of all Feudal Lords' Courts, was normally limited to disputes between its members, the King's tenants-in-chief, or to those cases which particularly concerned the King himself. The vast bulk of litigation was carried on in the old courts of shire and hundred, or in the newer Seignorial Tribunals. Not until the reign of Henry III was there any idea of the law of the King's Court becoming the Common Law. The ordinary freeman, who was not a tenant-in-chief, had access to it only in exceptional circumstances. Down to and including the reign of Henry I the royal writs covered perhaps three or four classes of civil case, and were not stereotyped. Their prerogatival nature was underlined by the fact that they could be obtained only from the King's Chancery, or

[1] F. W. Maitland, *Outlines of Legal History, Collected Papers,* Vol. II.
[2] F. M. Stenton, *Anglo-Saxon England,* 2nd Ed. 1947, Oxford, Clarendon Press, pp. 502–4 and 643.

secretariat, which at that time accompanied him wherever he might go. If he were abroad, as he frequently was, for long periods, the seeker after royal justice had to follow him overseas.

Early in the reign of Henry II, however, or perhaps late in that of Henry I, the decisive step was taken which made inevitable the centralization of civil justice in a royal court. An ordinance seems to have been issued declaring that no man should be impleaded of his freehold without a royal writ. Then it was ordained that all pleas "touching the freehold", and all personal pleas involving property worth more than forty shillings must be initiated in the County Court by writ and not by plaint—i.e. before the plaintiff could get his case heard at all he had to get a royal order entitling him to do so. Then a new writ was invented—the writ of 'pone', so called from its first word—which provided, like the probably older writ of 'recordari', that pleas in the County Court could be transferred to the King's Court at the request of the plaintiff.[1] A little later, possibly in 1166, came the Assize of Novel Disseisin, which ordained that anyone who had been dispossessed of his freehold could seek his remedy in the Royal Court, and abide the verdict of a jury of neighbours. The King had now definitely established himself as the protector of freehold. He was enabled to do this without difficulty by reason of the fact that he could provide a better and more rational procedure than that available to the ancient courts of shire and hundred or to seignorial justice, by his use of the jury. Other courts were limited to the ordeals, oath helping, or trial by battle. Only the King could compel men to swear to answer truthfully any question that might be put to them. The application of the jury to the trial of ordinary civil disputes was gradual, and was effected partly by a series of Assizes or Ordinances, the first and chief or which was the Assize of Novel Disseisin, dealing with particular classes of cases concerning freehold property, and also, imperceptibly, by the establishment of the principle that if in any action the parties came to an issue of fact—not of law—that issue might, if they agreed, be decided by a jury of neighbours.

Why did the King thus take freehold—and more also—under his special protection? Maitland says that Henry II was determined to make royal justice supreme in order to gain both power and money. Certainly the centralization of justice was a great step to-

[1] *Brevia Placitata,* Selden Society, ed. G. J. Turner and T. F. T. Plucknett, 1951, Introduction p. LXVIII.

wards the creation of a national monarchy, and was as great a spanner thrust into the working of the feudal machine as the sheriff or the fyrd, or even a greater one. Also "Justitia est magnum emolumentum". It seems possible, however, that there was an additional reason. The King's Peace, which had expanded after the Conquest till it had become the general safeguard of public order, was undoubtedly threatened by badly administered land laws. Difficulties in obtaining or regaining possession of land inevitably cause fighting, rioting, bloodshed and feud among a turbulent agricultural population. Henry II wanted to be able to go to France whenever he wished and to stay there for years at a time should that seem necessary. It was desirable that he should leave a comparatively peaceful and orderly England behind him.

The progressive centralization of justice was obviously too much for the Curia Regis, occupied with other business, and composed of a rather haphazard collection of barons and bishops. In 1178 five whole-time judges were appointed, three clerks and two laymen, who would dispose of the bulk of civil judicial work, but who were to reserve cases of unusual difficulty or novelty to the King and his Council.

The way was now open for the gradual development of an ordered legal system based upon the royal writs. These rapidly increased in number, especially during the reign of Henry III. The Chancery ceased to accompany the King on his travels, and seekers after royal justice had to go no further than Westminster. The existing writs soon became stereotyped, and were sold to litigants at a fixed price. Up till about the middle of the thirteenth century the King could and did produce new writs to cover new classes of litigation, and these were more expensive. But it then began to be realized that the King and his Chancery staff were in fact unobtrusively making new law, and that the centralization of justice, especially in the then all-important field of freehold property, was reducing the feudal courts, as well as the old courts of shire and hundred, to impotence. As early as 1216 the King had been forced by the baronage to cease the issue of the writ *Praecipe*, which simply ordered the defendant to return the land in dispute to the plaintiff, and if he did not do so, to appear in the King's Court and explain the reasons for his failure to obey the royal command. This writ had the effect of depriving Seignorial Courts of jurisdiction on disputes about land among the lords' own tenants. It caused the lord "to lose his court", and also the profits accruing therefrom, and was resented. By 1244 Henry III's steady expansion of the scope of royal justice caused fresh complaints, and demands were made that the Chancellor should be sworn to issue no more writs without the consent of the Council. This demand was incorporated in the Provisions of Oxford of 1258. Both the Council of Magnates and, later, the Parliament, appear to have thought that the Royal, or Common, Law had reached its full permissible development. So by Edward I's reign the series of royal commands came to a premature end. Where there was no writ there was no remedy at Common Law until one was provided by Statute, which was seldom. Naturally efforts were made, often by transparent fictions, or by the most forced interpretations, to make the existing writs fit instruments for work which they had not been designed to do. A mass of commentary, packed with legal learning, refined distinctions, and ingenious reconciliations, grew up around each writ. There were in all between thirty and forty, and possibly some hundreds of minor variations, some of which were issued by the Chancellor *in consimili casu* which was as far as the framers of the Statute of Westminster II in 1285 would go to miti-gate the inconveniences manifestly caused by the abrupt cessation of normal growth.[1]

Maitland, perhaps reluctantly, has summed up the results. The Law of England, he said, might well become an ingenious but tortuous commentary on ancient writs and statutes, "an occult science, a black art, a labyrinth of which the clue has been lost".[2]

The vast majority of the original writs were concerned with rights in land and the incidents of tenure. As trade increased, almost incredible ingenuity was exercised to make them applicable to other classes of litigation, but the difficulties of adapting a highly developed and intricate, but prematurely fixed, land law to the varied needs of commerce are obvious.[3] It is surprising not that it was not done well, but that it could be done at all.

New developments made necessary by the increasing needs of

[1] Some of these, however, notably the offshoots of 'trespass' gradually displaced the older forms of action almost entirely, and were capable of unrestricted variation in content.

[2] Pollock and Maitland, *History of English Law*, 2nd Ed., Cambridge 1911, Vol. I, p. 225.

[3] "The older English land law was as intricate and elaborately artificial a body of rules as the world has ever seen." Development of the Common Law, James Bryce, *Law Quarterly Review*, Vol. XXIV, 1908, p. 17.

rapidly advancing civilization, both in the law of contract and in that of personal property, had to be extracted, theoretically at any rate, from the intricate meshes of land tenure. As late as the middle of the seventeenth century Simonds D'Ewes wrote that Littleton's Tenures (c. 1480) was "the very key, as it were, of our common law, and accounted the most absolute work that was ever written touching it".[1] 'Coke upon Littleton' is the classic example of the enduring dominance of the land law. He describes the 'Tenures' as "the ornament of the Common Law and the most perfect work of its kind".[2] In commenting on Littleton's definition of a tenant in fee simple, Coke wrote "Littleton here and in many places, puts lands but for an example; for his rule extends to seignories, rents, advowsons, commons, estovers, and other hereditaments of what kind and nature soever", and goes on to say "Hereditament is the largest word of all in that kind; for whatever may be inherited is an hereditament, be it corporeal or incorporeal, real, personal, or mixed."[3]

"Out of the old fields must come the new corn" as Coke frequently insisted. Why was this extraordinary restriction accepted? Why were judges and lawyers content for hundreds of years to allow civil justice to writhe and twist in the shackles of the mediaeval land law? It seems that the reason is to be found in the habit of mind induced by their education.

[1] *Autobiography and Correspondence of Sir Simonds D'Ewes, Bart.*, ed. J. O. Halliwell, London 1845, Vol. I, p. 181.
[2] *Coke upon Littleton*, ed. Thomas Coventry, London 1845, Coke's Preface, p. XLV.
[3] *Coke upon Littleton*, Bk. I, Chap. I, § 1.

CHAPTER III

THE DEVELOPMENT OF COMMON LAW PROCEDURE

THE founders of Common Law procedure and practice, and after them generations of professional lawyers, were well educated men, unlike the King and his lay magnates, and the features of the system they devised, including its hampering restrictions, may be traced to the nature of that education. Mediaeval learning was based on the old Trivium of the Dark Ages—grammar (i.e. Latin), rhetoric, and above all logic, or dialectic (the two terms are interchangeable in the Middle Ages). The mediaeval student knew nothing of historical or comparative scholarship, nor was he concerned with observation. That, generally speaking, he considered to have been done. The key to all knowledge was to be found in the existing pronouncements of recognized authorities. The instrument used for their detailed investigation was dialectic, based on Aristotelian logic, whereby fallacious notions could be eliminated, the real meaning of the words discovered, and illustrations of the truth therein enshrined, and its application infallibly deduced. Generally speaking, all knowledge was deductive. Dialectic, culminating in public disputations conducted in accordance with the strictest syllogistic method—major premise, minor premise, conclusion—was the intellectual passion of the age. The absolute reverence for written authority made the syllogistic method readily practical and satisfying. It was necessary to have an authority regarded as axiomatic, behind which one could not go, or at least a statement clearly deducible from such an authority, as the foundation of one's major premise. One could not, for example, question the Bible, or even the Sentences of Peter Lombard, in theology, or Aristotle in philosophy, or Hippocrates in medicine. The same reverence came to be extended to the innumerable authors of glosses upon these primary authorities. Even medicine did not escape.[1] In time the most admired feat of the dialectician

---

[1] "In Paris medical training was along scholastic lines; the learned doctors preferred to dispute about diseases in impeccable syllogisms rather than examine a live patient infected with a real disease." Nathan Schachner, *The Mediaeval Universities,* University Press, Edinburgh 1938, p. 98.

was to demonstrate by syllogism—or rather by a concatenation of syllogisms—the truth of what to the untutored reason was obviously false or absurd, and this did not come to an end when Duns was put into Bocardo, but continued throughout the sixteenth century, and even into the seventeenth. Rashdall has summed up the defects of mediaeval education by saying that it was at once too dogmatic and too disputatious, and that the fundamental fault was the fatal indifference to facts, the facts of external nature, of history and of life. Mental vigour and acuteness were however by no means lacking, and 'though words were allowed to usurp the place of things, they were not allowed to usurp the place of thought'. The scholastic method of verbal scholarship provided a training in analytic subtlety which has perhaps never been surpassed.[1]

It was moreover not unsuitable for the study and interpretation of existing codes of law, and Law was the leading faculty in most of the universities of Europe. The study of both the Civil and the Canon Laws provided a severe intellectual discipline, a rigorous training in exact classification and definition, and in the recognition of minute distinctions.

But the scholastic method was not well adapted to the construction of a new legal system out of inadequate materials.

The unknown persons who founded the Inns of Court copied, however, the contemporary university curriculum closely and inevitably. The 'Readings' seem to have been conducted very much on the same lines as a formal lecture in the Schools; the 'moots' resembled the public disputations of advanced students. The basis of all knowledge was the corpus of writs, most of which dealt with the land law, and which stood in the place of the Bible for students of theology. Then the great mass of Patristic literature, 'The Fathers', which formed the case law of the theologian, containing many discrepancies and contradictions in urgent need of reconciliatory interpretation, was represented by the 'Year Books'. These were collections of probably more or less unofficial reports of cases, or parts of cases, intended, in the main, to illustrate and exemplify what could be done under the rules of pleading and procedure applicable to each form of action. They were taken down in court by legal practitioners in the archaic Norman French which had become the language of legal proceedings and legal literature.

[1] Hastings Rashdall, *The Universities of Europe in the Middle Ages,* ed. F. M. Powicke and A. B. Emden, Vol. III, p. 453.

Comparatively few decisions were quoted, and the discovery or application of general principles appeared to be of little interest to the reporters. They were chiefly concerned with the arguments of counsel and the remarks of individual judges on points of procedure and interpretation, a knowledge of which would be likely to assist a practising advocate in the actual conduct of a case. Printed editions of some of these Collections were published as early as the end of the fifteenth century.

The Year Books were the source of precedents, which were essentially necessary. Judges and lawyers were by the habit of mind induced by their education most chary of taking any responsibility whatever. They had an almost superstitious reverence for the *littera scripta*, and always needed some authority on which to base their arguments and speculations. The basic authority of the writs themselves did not help them much, except in cases of contravention of their terms or a mistaking of their content. They were useless for the formulation of arguments on points of procedure, which were often, if not usually, more vital for the decision of a case than points of substance.

The first forecasting of the English system of case law is to be found in the *Dialogus de Scaccario*, written some time at the end of the twelfth century by Richard of Ely, the Treasurer, who had held various judicial appointments, including that of a Justice of the Common Pleas. "There are," he said, "cases where the causes of events, and the reasons for decisions are obscure; and in these it is enough to cite precedents, particularly those derived from men of sense, whose actions are cautious, and founded on reason."[1] Bracton (c. 1265) collected some hundreds of them, but they do not appear to have been regularly quoted till well on in the reign of Edward I. They did not, however, become absolutely binding until the sixteenth century, when decisions began to be reported instead of arguments.

It is not proposed to enter into a discussion of the merits and demerits of case law. But it is clear that where law is being gradually made through the decision of cases, and the creation of precedents, its development, depending upon the classes of case brought before the courts, is bound to be uneven. Certainly the overwhelming predominance of the land law throughout the Middle Ages greatly exaggerated this inevitable defect. As Pollock said, "Few persons

[1] *Dialogus de Scaccario,* ed. A. Hughes, C. G. Crump, and Johnson, Oxford 1902, Introduction, XVII, XVIII.

C

who have not made a special study of the law can have any notion of the wonderfully uneven manner in which its growth has proceeded."[1] He wrote in 1882 that "England is the one country in Western Europe where it is most difficult for a man who is not a lawyer by profession to have any clear notion of the laws he lives under, and where the chances are greatest that matters of serious importance will turn out to be provided for inadequately or not at all."[2] This was even truer of the England of the fifteenth, sixteenth, and seventeenth centuries. Throughout that period (and after it) not only were the precedents more restricted in scope, and more hampered by the premature fixation, but immensely detailed, development of feudal land law, but they were recorded in a language which was quite unintelligible to the ordinary educated man.

Presumably the reason why Norman French and not Latin became the language of the legal profession was that it was the language of the Kings' own Court, to which cases from the Common Bench were occasionally referred. Normally neither the King nor his lay magnates could understand Latin. Then the Court Coram Rege (King's Bench), which eventually became an entirely professionalized Court of Common Law, but which for long did not lose its intimate connection with the King and his Council, naturally used French. English was in any case an impossible alternative in the twelfth and thirteenth centuries—a vulgar dialect, or group of dialects, wholly unfitted for the elaboration of technical exactitude. So, apart from the most formal documents, such as writs, which were always written in Latin, Norman French became the lawyers' language, and the language of the law. By the middle of the fourteenth century, if not before, few other than trained lawyers could understand it, and in 1362 a statute was passed ordering that henceforward pleas should be pleaded in English. The statute was not observed. Litigants were by no means always present in person and were not normally eligible as witnesses if they were. The evidence of witnesses was comparatively rarely taken till well on in the fifteenth century. Normally the lawyer sought to prove his case by verbal ingenuity, by quoting precedents, and by picking holes in his adversary's presentation, until a final issue of fact or law was reached. So the fact that no one but the judges and the lawyers could understand the pleadings did not appear to be a serious inconvenience.

[1] F. Pollock, *Essays in Jurisprudence and Ethics*, London 1882.
[2] Ibid., p. 63.

The teaching and practice of the law had become completely professionalized, and Norman French had become the professional language, in which alone legal minutiae could be logically and precisely expressed. Its exactness and technicality went on developing throughout the fourteenth and fifteenth centuries, until it came to pass that "the law in its full perfection was known only to some dozen men, the King's Justices".[1] "Law", said Maitland, "is the point where life and logic meet."[2] "But", said Holdsworth, "if the lawyers habitually use a highly abstract and a highly technical language, which because it is abstract and technical, is incapable of the slightest change, both the law and the language will tend to lose touch with common life. Life will be sacrificed to logic, and the lawyers will tend to become the slaves of their own abstractions."[3]

The progressive refinement and hardening of technicality, the fact that jurisprudence was becoming a voluminous commentary on formulae—i.e. writs—and above all the conduct of legal proceedings in a highly specialized professional language, rapidly made it impossible for any but a trained Common lawyer either to conduct business in the courts, or to act as a judge in civil cases. This happened much earlier in England than in Scotland. Civilians (i.e. those learned in the law of Rome) and canonists were, as such, completely unqualified, and a class of lay lawyers skilled in English legal learning began to appear as early as the reign of Edward I, or even earlier. Some time in that reign the legal profession began to be unified by the placing of these professional pleaders and attorneys under the control of the judges. Before long the new profession of what we should now call Common lawyers had established a complete monopoly of all legal business. The provision of a highly specialized legal education became necessary. This could not be obtained in the universities, still in England mainly ecclesiastical, though an ineffectual effort to supply the demand was made in Oxford in the fifteenth century. The Roman and Canon laws only were taught there, and Latin was the sole medium of instruction, so what was in practice a new university, the Inns of Court and Inns of Chancery, where law French could be learned, was founded, or rather, perhaps, grew up, at some time—probably fairly early—in the fourteenth century. Fortescue, Chief Justice of the King's Bench.

[1] Pollock and Maitland, *History of English Law*, Vol. I, p. 224.
[2] *Year Books of 1 and 2 Edward II*, Selden Society, ed. F. W. Maitland, Introduction.
[3] Holdsworth, *History of English Law*, Vol. II, p. 482.

gave in his *De Laudibus Legum Angliae* a detailed account of the life
and work of students in the Inns of Court in the fifteenth century.
As it was in his day, so it remained practically unchanged for generations. He says that at least two hundred students belonged to each
of the Inns of Court. In addition at least one hundred attended each
of the ten Inns of Chancery where the elements of law were taught.
In term-time the students flocked to the courts at Westminster,
where they listened to the trial of cases.[1]

By the beginning of the fifteenth century a definite legal hierarchy
had been established, at the head of which were the sergeants at law,
selected by the Crown, and the Judges, who by this time were re-
cruited solely from the sergeants. Below these were the Benchers of
the Inns; the Readers; the Ancients; the Utter, or Outer, barristers,
who were practising advocates; and the Inner barristers, or students,
all of which classes were graded as "apprentices" in the Inns of
Court and Chancery. No one was admitted to the rank of sergeant
who had not completed at least sixteen years of 'apprenticeship'.
Only sergeants could appear in the Court of Common Pleas. It is
not surprising that so detailed and long drawn out a training in what
Coke rightly called "the artificial reason of the law" should have
resulted, as Erasmus said, in lawyers becoming 'the most unlearned
sort of learned men'. They knew, or the best of them knew, the
intricate rules of process and pleading extremely well, but little else.

These rules were of extraordinary complication, and by the later
fifteenth century contained provisions which the passage of time
had rendered obsolete or even unintelligible. 'Mesne process'—the
art of producing a defendant in court—was excessively dilatory.
Every opportunity was given to the reluctant defendant to postpone
his appearance, and keep his adversary or his adversary's lawyer
hanging about the offices of the court, spending his money on obtaining writs of distraint, or of arrest; awaiting their return, and feeing
clerks. Judicial writs of all kinds were limited in operation to a
single shire, and could be served only through the Sheriff.[2] Apart
from 'Sheriff's tricks' (Sheriff's offices were foci of corruption) such

---

[1] Sir John Fortescue, *De Laudibus legum Angliae*, ed. S. B. Chrimes, Cap. XLVIII,
p. 117.

[2] "First one wrytt may serve but for one shyre; as though the King were lord but
of one shyre! But I demand, why may not one wrytt serve in all shyres, yea, in all
placys under the Kyng's dominion, wheresoever he or hys may find his defendant?
Surely there is no godly reason why to the contrary, but even the only private welth
of sotle lawyers. And, as farre as I can lerne, one wrytt lasteth but for one terme; and

as the losing, deliberate non service, or non return of writs, all manner of 'essoins' or excuses for failure to appear were allowed. An infant might be impleaded and the case adjourned till he or she came of age; or a royal protection, issued on behalf of someone who was on the King's service, might cause an adjournment *sine die*. Essoins ceased to be of major importance in the fifteenth century, but the difficulty of getting a writ served on a defendant remained throughout the period, and the task of securing his appearance might still be a formidable one. There were two main types of process, by distraint of property, or by the arrest, and if necessary outlawry, of the defendant. Both were highly complex, and in the absence of good communications, inevitably slow. It has been estimated that process by arrest and outlawry took in the most favourable circumstances at least one and a half years, and much longer if the defendant were determined and influential. Process by distraint might be fairly quick, if the defendant came to heel at the first distress. But if he lasted out even when all his property—or such of it as could be found—had gone, and the defendant had to resort to the alternative method of arrest and outlawry, several years might elapse. The plea rolls are very largely occupied by entries of mesne process. In some terms they amount to as much as five-sixths of the total number of entries.[1] A large number of cases reported in the Year Books turn on the intricate manoeuvres which these rules made possible. Holdsworth regards them as the least reasonable part of the mediaeval (and later than mediaeval) Common Law, and considers that the breakdown of administration in the fifteenth century was in large part due to them.[2]

Then, when at long last the parties—or their lawyers—confronted

---

the next terme he must be at charge to come up, or at least to send sometime iii or iv hundred myle for another. Agayne, no man may serve it but the Sheryff of the shyre or his man, and so many times it is sure that the sheryff or his man (and sometyme both) playe the false shrewys in geving the party warning to kepe him out of the way, or to go into another shyre. Oh, the unnumerable wyles, craftys, sotyltes and delayes that be in the lawe, which the lawyers will never spye, because of their private lucres sake." Henry Brinklow's *Complaint of Roderyck Mors*, ed. J. Meadows Cooper, Early English Text Society 1874 (*c.* 1542), Cap. VII, p. 20. Also see N. Neilson in Ch. VIII of *The English Government at Work 1327–1336*, Vol. III, ed. W. H. Dunham, Mediaeval Academy of America, Cambridge, Mass., 1950. He says that adjournments owing to the failure of the sheriff to return the writ was the chief cause of the great delays in justice.

[1] Margaret Jennings, *The Court of Common Pleas in XVth Century England*, New York, Cornell University Press, 1947, Cap, XII.

[2] Holdsworth, *History of English Law*, Vol. III, p. 626.

each other, the unique law of pleading, which had developed during the fourteenth and fifteenth centuries tended to make the outcome of a case depend more on the technical excellence—or the reverse—of its presentation, than on its merits. The aim was to isolate a single issue of law or of fact, on the decision of which judgement would be awarded, by a prolonged and precise logical process. If the issue finally arrived at were one of law, it was decided by the judge; if of fact, by the verdict of a jury. This dichotomy was primarily due to the predominating influence of the land law.

Not only had the complicated labour to be undertaken of making new types of corn grow from fields the soil of which was entirely unsuitable for their cultivation, but their harvesting had very frequently to be done with the ancient agricultural implement. It is true that the use of the jury had advantages. Where there was no overbearing local influence, and no faction feeling, a jury of neighbours was a suitable body for the settlement of questions of fact about the ownership or possession of land, and also the incidents of tenure, in their own villages. They could be expected to possess the detailed and accurate local knowledge required.

But ignorant and illiterate people were not equipped to decide complicated questions of accounts, or contracts or to understand the thousand and one ramifications of commercial relationships.

The rules of pleading were therefore developed in the fourteenth and fifteenth centuries mainly with a view to reducing the case, however intricate it might be, to a single simple issue which a jury could or might understand, or to a single issue of law, on which the judge could arrive at a decision without an intolerable expenditure of time and labour.[1] But as both the subject matter of litigation and the law itself had become more complicated in the fifteenth century than in the thirteenth and fourteenth, it was sometimes undesirable to leave the decision to a jury, even when the point at issue was clearly a question of fact. The solution evolved was typical of English legal methods. Any drastic change was unthinkable. So the doctrine of 'colour' was invented about the middle of the fifteenth century. Facts were admitted, and, as a rule, invented, which would give rise to a question of law, and the judge then took over.[2]

[1] See Hayes' Dialogue, quoted in Appendix I of Holdsworth, Vol. IX, "That might be all very well if people went to law for the convenience of the judges and juries and not to get justice for themselves".

[2] Holdsworth, *History of English Law*, Vol. IX, pp. 299 et seq.

It will be observed that this method of pleading was worked out in order to expedite the doing of reasonable justice with the tools available. But "the issue was not answerable to the simplicity and honesty of the design."[1] It is true that what was known as "the general issue" could be pleaded in certain classes of case. This was simply a contradiction *in toto* of the plaintiff's allegations, and the effect of it was that the case came at once before the court and was decided on its merits. In the majority of cases, however, special pleading was necessary, and the process by which the final single issue was ultimately arrived at was refined and elaborated by the ruthless application of pure dialectical method, and became an exact science of extraordinarily minute and subtle technicality. The defects of this development were obvious enough, but were outweighed by the lawyers' delight in the scope it gave to the elaboration of logical technique. It did not reach full perfection till the sixteenth century, when the system of written pleadings drawn up by the lawyers of each side outside the court was introduced. Before that the pleadings had been oral and were made in the presence of the judge.[2] Though the extreme elaboration of the later method was not attained, and the number of fatal procedural pitfalls was not so great, a high degree of formal accuracy was always necessary. Each of the forms of action—i.e. the actions which it was possible to bring under an original writ—required strict adherence to the detailed rules of pleading applicable to it. The choice of the wrong writ on which to base a claim, or a mistake in the pleadings—e.g. pleading outside the content of the writ—meant the instant dismissal of the suit. 'Duplicity', which means not deceitfulness, but pleading or attempting to plead more than one issue, was at once fatal, even though a clear miscarriage of justice would result.[3] Moreover the pleas had to be enrolled, and owing to the sanctity of the written word, which persisted till the nineteenth century, the record was

---

[1] O. Cromwell, *Letters & Speeches*, ed. T. Carlyle, 3rd ed., p. 276

[2] It was probably to save the time of the judges that the written system was adopted, as by it the judge did not see the case at all until the issue had been framed.

[3] See *An Early Admiralty Case*, Camden Miscellany, Vol. XV, 1929, for an attempt by Common Lawyers to get the rule adopted there. The defendant, a Frenchman, pleaded (i) that the capture of 'the St. Mary boat' was an act of war; (ii) that if a truce had been proclaimed he had no knowledge of it; (iii) that the treaty of Bretigny barred claims for capture during the war.

The defendants demurred on the ground of 'multiplicity', but the Admiralty Court held that it was not bound by the rules of Common Law, but must administer equity.

incontrovertible, normally incapable of the slightest amendment, and therefore proof positive of what the proceedings had been. Even a trifling verbal slip or omission was decisive, unless it could be rectified by the provisions of one or other of the statutes of Jeofail, and no judgment could be given for the plaintiff even if he had gained his case. If the judgment had been pronounced before the mistake in the record had been discovered, it could be reversed on a writ of error. The introduction of the written system of pleadings greatly enlarged the scope of this rule.

It may perhaps be reasonable to suppose that the "incognoscibility" of the Common Law was in part responsible for not only the preservation but the extension of the sacramental importance of verbal accuracy, and for the decisive weight given to logical correctness in procedure. It was certainly often easier to decide a case upon some obvious procedural flaw than to discover, or deduce, the substantive law on the point. But procedural forms were a part of the law, and from fairly early in the fourteenth century there was no element of equity to allow the correction of a false step in the maze they had become.

CHAPTER IV

THE DISAPPEARANCE OF EQUITY

MUCH has been written about the disappearance of equitable principle from the King's Courts which had been brought into existence partly, at any rate, to supply it, though the full extent of the calamity has rarely, if ever, been recognized by historians.

There was for some time every likelihood of the adoption of genuinely equitable modifications of purely legal rigidity owing to the infiltration of ideas drawn from the Roman and Canon laws. In Roman jurisprudence law and equity had been fused. "In omnibus quidem, maxime tamen in jure, aequitas spectanda sit." What was not Roman in the Canon Law was Christian, so both laws, being unchallengeably authoritative, were saved from the disaster which befell the Common Law of England. To begin with, many of the Common Law judges were ecclesiastics—men like Bracton, learned in Italian jurisprudence. Though probably none of them were trained Canonists, all would have had some general knowledge of the basic principles of the Canon Law, and particularly of the stress laid on the operation of conscience. While they remained equity could not be entirely eliminated, and recognition of the necessity for a measure of elasticity in the administration of justice did come creeping in, in spite of the highly restrictive influence of writ and precedent.

Up to the close of the second decade of the fourteenth century, attempts were still occasionally made to temper the rigid application of rules when it was clear that injustice would result. Chief Justice Bereford, of the Common Pleas (who, strangely enough, was a layman) several times endeavoured to do so. In 1318 he went so far as to hold a writ good on the ground that, though it did not adequately represent the plaintiff's case,[1] there was no other form in Chancery which suited it better. In 1319 he was reported as saying "a plea of account shall not be conducted by Common Law, but by equity and reason."[2] His views, however, in spite of his influen

[1] *Year Book 12, Edward II, 1318*, Selden Society, 1946.
[2] *Year Book 12, Edward II, 1319*, Seldon Society, 1951.

tial position and his long experience (he had been a judge of the
Common Bench since 1291) were not approved or copied. When
once in the name of good faith he urged defendant's counsel to
admit a claim that had not been proved, back came the retort
"You must not allow conscience to prevent your doing law".[1]
No ecclesiastic was appointed to be a judge after 1316. After their
day, and Bereford's, no vestige of genuine equity, understood as the
operation of conscience in legal proceedings, was allowed to remain,
and for more than five hundred years the country suffered from
having two legal systems, as the King was still bound to do equitable justice, and therefore to provide relief from the undiluted
rigour of the law, when it was clear that substantial justice had not
been done, or was unobtainable.

Apart from the short-lived influence of Roman jurisprudence,
it has often been assumed that genuinely equitable justice was
consciously administered in the eyre. After 1244, however, the
itinerant justices were invariably appointed from the Common
Bench. The advocates who accompanied them were, moreover,
always those who practised in that court. In short, the persons
employed on the eyre, both Bench and Bar, were the architects of
the Common Law system. It is scarcely credible that they left all
their working principles behind them at Westminster when they
became itinerant.

The advantage of the eyre to the ordinary small freeholder was
that for the remedy of most grievances he did not have to go to the
Chancery to find, or hire a lawyer to find, a writ which would or
might suit his case. He had merely to present a 'bill', or petition,
giving the substance of his plaint, written as a rule in extremely bad
Norman French. This was accepted, provided that it told a consistent and intelligible story. Many pitfalls, and much time and
expense, were thereby avoided.[2] This highly beneficial simplifica-
tion dates from the troubled years of 1258 and 1259. The serious
political unrest which then developed and which lasted till 1267 was
due in the main to high-handed and corrupt behaviour by local
officials, and also to the kindred problem of the failure of the
administration of the land law. It was necessary to enable ordinary

---

[1] *Year Books 1 & 2, Edward II, 1307–9*, Selden Society, 1903.
[2] Oxford Studies in Social and Legal History, Vol. VIII. *Studies in the Period of
Baronial Reform and Rebellion*, E. F. Jacob, Oxford 1925, Preface (Professor Vinogradoff) p. VI; and Introductory Note (E. F. Jacob), p. XII.

folk to get their complaints simply and speedily and cheaply before the court. Apart from this very substantial concession, the procedure of the eyre seems to have been exactly the same as at Westminster Hall. Though it must have been obvious that the waiving of the need for a writ automatically put out of court a whole class of technical pleadings, it seems doubtful whether the judges ever thought that they were administering equity and not law. It is however certain that, however dreaded the other manifestation of the eyre might be, its administration of civil justice was popular. Bolland's statement that the eyre was hated and feared by all men, and that it was merely a travelling branch of the Exchequer, whose object was not the doing of justice, but the levying of amercements on all and sundry, seems to be too sweeping.[1] From the middle of the thirteenth century no county was visited by the itinerant judges more than once in seven years, yet people, including Londoners, were content to wait till the next visitation to try to get their wrongs righted. The informal and inexpensive procedure by bill was adapted to the needs of small freeholders, and the eyre on its civil side was for most purposes the Court of Common Pleas for the majority of Englishmen entitled to sue at Common Law. The wealthy preferred to transact their business at Westminster Hall, and the villeins, still the great bulk of the population, were not concerned. Neither Westminster nor the eyre were for them.

This system, which undoubtedly did something to mitigate the growing rigour and expense of the law for the greater part of the litigating public, lasted for roughly one hundred years, and in its fully developed form for about thirty-five. Regular eyres ceased to be held after 1294. Why was the eyre abandoned? The main reason was presumably because other means now existed for the fulfilment of most of its functions. For some time presentments of the King's feudal dues and proprietary rights had been of no great importance, as Estreaters had been appointed to look after them. The judges of Assize visited the localities to deal with cases of Novel Disseisin and kindred matters.[2] Commissions of gaol delivery, on which there was no need to employ professional judges, could try criminals, and commissions of Trailbaston could be appointed to suppress serious disorders.

[1] W. C. Bolland, *The General Eyre*, Cambridge 1922.
[2] See *The English Government at Work 1327–36*, ed. W. A. Morris, W. H. Dunham and others, Mediaeval Academy of America, Cambridge, Mass., 1947–50, Cap. VII, Judges of Assize.

The cessation of the comparatively cheap and speedy trial of civil cases, other than those within the competence of the judges of Assize, and the obviating of a possibly long, expensive, and even dangerous journey to Westminster, was certainly a blow to the tenant farmer. But the richer landowners, feudal magnates, and holders of liberties and franchises, cordially disliked procedure by bill, which made it comparatively easy for their poorer neighbours to bring them into court.[1] It seems likely that the judges also, now that their system of writ and precedent had developed and hardened, joined forces with the aristocracy in persuading the King that there was no longer any need for modification of the full rigour of the game. There had been extensions of the law, notably in the actions of trespass, which were made to cover administrative grievances. These were definitely in the interests of the smaller tenant. Trained lawyers existed in sufficient numbers to assist ignorant people to run the full course of the law under Westminster rules, and the general lines of orthodox Common Law procedure were, or ought to have been, fully understood. Edward I may not have been at all difficult to persuade. He seems fully to have realized the advantages which "the subjecting subtlety" of law gave him,[2] and undoubtedly did much to make the legal profession a close corporation, and to centralize civil justice in the courts at Westminster. It was probably in his reign that the competence of the County Courts in money suits was limited to forty shillings.

Why were the beginnings of equitable reform so suddenly and completely extinguished?[3] Maitland believed that the cause was the hardening of accurately formulated case law, and there can be no doubt that the use of authoritative precedents, even though subtle distinction and verbal ingenuity might render them capable of more than one interpretation, must have tended to the development of formal rigidity, and to the exclusion from consideration of the purely individual merits of a case. Nor were equitable principles extractable from the Royal Writs on which the Common Law was based. It is also true that the older law, the influence of which was still potent, had been in no sense equitable. The scales were clearly weighted against equity. Nevertheless for some time the judges

---

[1] E. F. Jacob, op. cit., pp. 56 and 109.
[2] Lord Brooke, *Treatise of Monarchy*, ed. Grosart, Vol. I, § VII, line 239.
[3] *Pace* Professor Hazeltine, Review of Holdsworth's *History of English Law*, Vols. I–IV, *E.H.R.*, XL.

could and did administer equity and not merely writ bound and case bound law. This seems to militate against the conclusions of both Holdsworth and Adams that the doing of equitable justice being a peculiarly royal prerogative, the Courts of Common Law were not entitled to administer it after they had developed a quasi-independence and ceased to be intimately identified with the personal authority of the ruler. Adams thinks that the new central Court, the Common Bench, owed its disqualification to the fact that it was not an offshoot of the King's Council, but its creature, designed to exercise "a delegated jurisdiction strictly limited by the purposes for which the Court was created".[1] Not only does he ignore the fact that up to 1320 or thereabouts the exercise of equitable principles was not unknown to the judges of the Common Bench, but also he does not notice the fact that the judges 'coram Rege' who for long maintained intimate relations with the Council, and with the King in person, failed to develop or maintain an equitable jurisdiction. The Court of King's Bench did become simply a Court of Common Law, as did the Court of the Exchequer, but both were undeniably offshoots of the Council. The notion that the doing of substantial justice came to be expressly ruled out of the competence of the King's judges is unnatural, unsupported by any direct evidence, and, indeed, incredible. But there seems to be no doubt that it was ruled out, and was not a purely natural development from the growing number and extreme technical complexity of the forms and processes which were evolved, though they did tend inevitably to concentrate attention on their proper working, and to make justice a machine-made product. Who was responsible for making a tendency so early into an iron rule, which made a mistake in the handling of the machine fatal to the individual substance of the case put into it, however excellent it might be? It was not the King. Maitland recognizes that the judges themselves were responsible, but he gives no reason.[2]

It seems that the reason is to be found in the habit of mind induced by the education of the lay judges, who had come to regard the law of Rome with contempt, and the rival system of the Canonists with dislike and jealousy. The elimination of equity from the Common Law was the direct consequence of English legal training, which was

[1] G. B. Adams, *Councils and Courts in Anglo-Norman England*, Yale Historical Publications, 1926, p. 219.
[2] Pollock and Maitland, *History of English Law*, Vol. II, p. 563.

itself the child of mediaeval scholasticism, and followed naturally from a system which had been devised with meticulous care over a long period of years to give legally correct and authoritative answers. Such a system, wholly deductive in its essence, could not be upset by the necessity for considering the unforeseeable vagaries of human affairs and conduct. The operation of conscience was anathema. The claim of the Common Lawyers in their battle with the equitable jurisdiction of the Chancery was always that decisions reached by way of the Common Law were 'certain'.[1] In practice no one normally had the slightest degree of certainty that a case was legally sound until the judge pronounced his decree. What was meant was that whatever the decision might be, it was not dependent upon the opinion evolved by any particular individual from his inner consciousness—or conscience—but was certainly deduced from authoritative precedents, and the principles enshrined in them. What it would actually be depended upon which of the mass of precedents the judge chose to rely on, and on the interpretation which he chose to give them. Whether the answer were 'yes' or 'no', it was still 'certain'. But, as the author of 'A Replication of a Sergeante at the Lawes of England' wrote, sometime about 1530, in protest against the Chancellor's interference with the due course of the law, "Conscience is a thing of great uncertaintie, for some men thinke that if they treade upon two straws that lie across, that they offend in conscience, and some man thinketh that if he lake money, and another hath too moche, he may take part of his with conscience; and so, diverse men, diverse consciences."[2] As in the universities, so in the Inns of Court, ruthless dialectical rigour tended to restrict the exercise of common sense, and not to allow an ordinary knowledge of affairs to muddy the pure springs of ratiocination. No 'desultory and uncertain remedies' dictated by so vague and variable a deter-

[1] Chief Justice Vaughan said in his judgment on Bushell's case (1670): "I would know whether anything be more common than for two men, students, barristers, or judges, to deduce contrary and opposite conclusions out of the same case in law".

[2] *Hargreaves Tracts, 1787.* A hundred years later Selden said "Equity is a roguish thing; for in law we have a measure—know what to trust to; equity is according to the conscience of him that is Chancellor, and as that is larger or narrower, so is equity. It is all one as if they should make the standard for the measure we call a foot, a Chancellor's foot; what an uncertain measure would this be? One Chancellor has a long foot, another a short foot; a third an indifferent foot; it is the same thing in the Chancellor's conscience." *Selden's Table Talk*, edition of 1821, p. 52.

But surely it would be a mistake for a cobbler to use the same last for everyone's foot.

minant as conscience, or an unanalysed instinct of fair play, were conceivable. They had to be certainly deducible from recognized authority.

Great skill and ingenuity had been displayed in the construction of the uniquely scholastic English system. Even in modern times it is observable that those scholars who were best acquainted with the subtleties of the Common Law grew to admire them, and to ignore the claims of equity to a share in the doing of justice, not because they hated justice and loved iniquity, but because to them on their intellectual side, logic had a stronger appeal than life. Maitland is an outstanding example. He was fully aware of the labyrinth the law had become. But he had the clue, and his informed admiration for the ingenuity of the maze made him appear to rejoice in the escape of England from a 'Reception', which to him implied "the pedantry that seeks to appropriate the law of another race, and galvanise a dead Corpus Juris into a semblance of life."[1] He did not consider in this regard the comparative success of the prerogative Courts, nor did he glance at the history of the law in Scotland, which, though it owes much to the Common Law, and uses juries in both criminal and civil cases, is largely drawn from the Corpus Juris through its derivative the Canon Law. At no time has the operation of the Courts in Scotland been a grievance and a stumbling-block to any section of the people. Had Maitland chosen to consider the results of a partial 'Reception' in Britain north of the Tweed, he might have been forced to the conclusion that the reason for the absence of any sign of rooted hostility to law and lawyers, so frequent in England from the fourteenth century to the nineteenth, so uninterrupted from Langland to Dickens, was due to the primary and vital fact that law and equity in Scotland have always been administered in the same courts.[2] But he finds the fact that the Common Law judges refused to be responsible for anything beyond an application of iron rules to be praiseworthy, and almost rejoices over their rejection of "the plausibly reasonable system of procedure which the Civilians and Canonists were constructing."[3] "High technique", he wrote, "is admirable whenever and wherever it is seen."[4]

[1] F. W. Maitland, *English Law and the Renaissance*.
[2] See Equity in Scots Law, David M. Walker, *Juridical Review*, Vol. LXVI, No. 2, August 1954, Edinburgh.
[3] Pollock and Maitland, Vol. II, p. 563.
[4] *Year Books 1 & 2*, ed. F. W. Maitland, Introduction, p. XVIII.

To sum up, by the second half of the fifteenth century, the Common Law had been administered, developed, and refined by a small group of highly trained professional lawyers, who were determined to make out of a bundle of ancient writs, a handful of statutes, and a heap of precedents, a judicial system which would stand comparison as a monument of legal science with the Law of Rome and the Canon Law. With the best intentions they had sought to render it more efficient by making it progressively more and more complicated. It could not be accepted that the answer ultimately arrived at by strict adherence to the intricate rules of process and procedure, coupled with the skilled interpretation of relevant precedents, would not always be the right one. If it was right legally it did not matter that it was often obviously unjust, any more than it mattered to the dialectician that his conclusion was practically absurd if it was, or appeared to be, syllogistically sound.

The centralization of justice had been carried to extreme limits, especially considering the badness of communications. Moreover the courts sat at Westminster for less than three months in the year, during the four terms of Hilary, Easter, Trinity and Michaelmas, each of which lasted for about three weeks. These short sessions, during which the judges sat for about three hours a day, naturally added greatly to the delays imposed by the rules of process and pleading.[1] Advocates and attorneys had to be engaged, as only they understood the working of the machine, and numerous clerks had to be fee'd for drawing up possibly large numbers of documents, and making entries in the rolls.

[1] Sir Thomas Smith, *De Republica Anglorum*, ed. L. Alston, London 1906. "This small time, and all that but in one place may seem very injurious to the people, who must be faine to suffer much wrong for lack of justice and of place and time to pleade." The only justification Sir Thomas Smith can find for it is Cato's opinion that "all the waies to the place of pleading were cast over with calthrops. He meant that they were but idle whoteheads, busie bodies and troublesome men in the Commonwealth that did so nourish pleading: good labourers and quiet men could bee content to ende their matters at home by judgment of their neighbours and kinsfolk, without spending so their money upon procurers and advocates, whom we call attornies, Counsellers, Sergeants and generallie men of lawe. Those he accounted profitable citizens who attend their honest labour and business at home, and not stande waiting and gaping upon their rolles and process in the lawe: as for the other by his judgment, it was no matter what mischief they suffered". Harrison seems to have agreed. The shortness of the law terms and the cost of law he said, "doth drive those often times to like of peace, who otherwise would live at strife, and quicklie be at ods".

W. Harrison, *Description of England*, ed. F. J. Furnivall, London 1877. Part I, Bk. 2, Cap. IX, *c.* 1570–80.

It is then not too much to say that, after the passing of the eyre, only the comparatively well-to-do could afford to seek remedies at Common Law. Even to them the long drawn uncertainty as to what the ultimately certainly deducible answer of the court would be must sometimes have been vexatious. It can often only have been the fierce and unscrupulous litigiousness of an age woefully deficient in amusements that drew even the wealthy to Westminster Hall.

CHAPTER V

THE CREATION AND DEVELOPMENT OF THE EQUITABLE JURISDICTION OF CHANCERY TILL THE END OF THE FIFTEENTH CENTURY

THE King and his Council still remained available, at any rate to the persistent suitor, whose rights the Common Law had been unable to protect. Just as the obligation of the King to do equitable justice to all men had permitted appeals to him against the failures of the old courts of shire and hundred, and the newer feudal tribunals, so, once the new system of royal justice had become professionalized, and the royal justices had succeeded in eliminating the idea of equitable dealing from the content of what had become the 'Common Law', the King was bound to intervene to correct the failures of the Royal Courts.

Naturally enough, owing to the abandonment of the eyre, the equitable jurisdiction of the King in Council rapidly increased in the fourteenth and early fifteenth centuries.[1] It seems to have sat in the Chancery for the hearing of cases between party and party. Though by imperceptible stages the exercise of prerogative justice in civil cases began to be handed over to the Chancellor as early as the reign of Richard II and possibly in that of Edward III, judgments by Chancellor and Council are found as late as the reign of Edward IV.[2] By the end of the fifteenth century the Court of the Chancellor had however become almost entirely distinct, and the King's Council had practically limited its judicial competence to cases in which the State was interested, and especially to those in which the maintenance of public order was at issue, rather than the disputes of private persons.[3] Holdsworth suggests that the authority given to the Chancellor by the Statute of Westminster II slightly to modify the forms of writ may help to explain why he came to be regarded as the official who could do justice when the Common Law could

[1] G. B. Adams, *Courts and Councils in Anglo-Norman England*, p. 203.

[2] *Select Cases in Chancery*, ed. W. F. Baildon, Selden Society, 1896, p. XV.

[3] Cases of outrage, however, occasionally came before the Chancellor down to the end of Elizabeth's reign, and cases of forcible seizure of property as late as that of Charles I.

provide no remedy.[1] Dicey considered that pressure of other business, and the difficulty of understanding cases involving some knowledge of legal procedure, led to the Council referring them to the Chancellor for decision, and this seems very much more likely.[2] Why to the Chancellor? It is suggested that the main reasons were firstly that the Chancellor, in virtue of his control of the issue of original writs, was the head of the English legal system; and secondly, that he was not a Common Lawyer, but almost always an ecclesiastic, and as such, to some extent at least, versed in the equitable principles of the Canon Law. He was also the chief member of the Council—"The King's natural Prime Minister", and he had an organized office. He was armed with the executive authority of Government, unlike the judges, whose powers of compulsion were weak and circumscribed, and he could obtain the presence of defendants comparatively easily and swiftly. He was therefore well equipped to become, as he was later described "the Keeper of the King's Conscience".

Up to the early part of the sixteenth century the sphere of the Chancellor was by no means clearly delineated. In theory application was to be made to him only when there was no remedy at Common Law. But "by the middle of the fifteenth century a plaintiff in Chancery can talk of 'the law of conscions, which ys law executory in the Courte for default of remedy by Courtes of the Common Law'."[3] 'Default of remedy' can be made to cover far more than 'absence of remedy', and there is no doubt that the Chancellor's discretion was extremely wide. Moreover, if he chose to assume jurisdiction the judges of the Common Law had no power to check him. No sustained effort was made to reform the Common Law until the sixteenth century, when a slow and piecemeal process of camouflaged modernization was begun. It was therefore inevitable that the encroachments of equity on what ought to have been Common Law territory were wide and deep. Holdsworth wrote "It is no exaggeration to say that by the middle of the fifteenth century the rules of the Common Law were either so perverted in their application, or so neglected, that they had ceased to protect adequately life and property."[4] The Chancellor therefore was often the

---

[1] Holdsworth, *History of English Law*, Vol. I, p. 398.
[2] A. V. Dicey, *Privy Council 1887*.
[3] *Select Cases in Chancery*, Selden Society, ed. W. F. Baildon, 1896, p. 146.
[4] Holdsworth, *History of English Law*, Vol. IV, p. 407.

only recourse of the afflicted, and it seems that whenever possible, or even when there was only the faintest hope of acceptance, an appeal was made to him. Chancery proceedings for the reigns of Richard II, Henry IV, Henry V, Henry VI, Edward IV and Richard III number well over a hundred thousand.[1] Much the greater part dates from the last three reigns, when the Chancellor, who was sole judge, must have been grievously overworked. During the turmoil of the fifteenth century, in addition to the longstanding defects in the content and machinery of the Common Law, legal process was constantly abused by the great and unscrupulous. Local officials were corrupted or overawed, and juries were regularly suborned. Maintenance, Champerty and conspiracy to defraud were rampant. The Common Law was not equipped to deal with any of these closely connected offences. It seems that that no writ of conspiracy existed at Common Law, and it is doubtful whether there were Common Law writs for either Champerty or Maintenance. Statutes there were, but their application was restricted, and also curiously perverted. False accusations were so frequent that the courts were apt to take action for maintenance or conspiracy against anyone coming forward voluntarily as a witness. People were therefore afraid to do so, and frequently petitioned the Chancellor to order them to appear, in which case they would be immune. As Winfield says, "it took a very long time to solve the legal puzzle of punishing the rogue who would kill and rob with the law's own weapons without at the same time terrifying the honest accuser or plaintiff."[2] The writ under the statute was also inapplicable even in the clearest case if the person complaining had not been actually tried and acquitted.[3]

Applications to the Chancellor by the oppressed were therefore numerous, and he frequently intervened. But the executive power of the Government had dwindled away, and he could probably often do little more than prevent some at least of the baseless claims and charges from coming before the Courts of Common Law. Con-

[1] W. T. Barbour, *History of Contract in Early English Equity*. Oxford Studies in Social and Legal History, Vol. IV, Oxford 1914. Preface by Paul Vinogradoff, p. IV.

[2] P. H. Winfield, Cambridge Studies in English Legal History. *History of Conspiracy and Abuse of Legal Procedure*, 1921.

[3] Richard III summoned all the judges and asked them whether if anyone had brought a false writ and action against another whereby he is imprisoned and dies in prison, there would be any remedy for the party or the King. The justices replied that there would be none, since the action was not ended. The trial had not been completed and the unfortunate man had therefore not been acquitted. *Year Book 2 Richard III*, quoted by P. H. Winfield, op. cit., p. 88.

spiracy and its congeners were ultimately defeated by the King's Council in the Star Chamber after the royal authority had been re-established, not by the Chancellor sitting as sole judge.

Apart from cases arising from the misconduct of the overmighty subject, which were not very numerous until well on in the fifteenth century, the main classes of suit dealt with by the Chancellor immediately after the establishment of his separate jurisdiction were those which could not be tried by the ordinary courts, because there was no provision in the law under which they could be entertained, or those which had failed at Common Law merely owing to the rigidity of its rules, and the limitations of their application.

Perhaps the most important class in the first category was that of uses and trusts. These were not recognized by the Common Law, and the dishonest or defaulting feoffee to uses was immune until the Chancellor stepped in in the name of equity and good conscience.[1] An almost equally vital deficiency was the impossibility of getting specific performance of contractual obligations at Common Law. Damages only could be obtained by the successful plaintiff, though what he wanted was the actual land which was to have been conveyed to him by a contract of sale, or the return of a specific chattel which for one reason or another was of particular value to him. The Chancellor could order specific performances, and appeals to him to do so were numerous. The ordinary courts were also almost incapable of dealing with matters of account—except when guardians or receivers were concerned, or in cases in which the bailiffs of landlords had failed to render reasonable account of sums collected by them. The Common Law writ of account was applicable only when the transactions concerned had taken place in England, so the important and increasing class of cases arising from foreign trade were automatically ruled out of consideration. It is also obvious that a jury, which was the only resort of the Common Law for the decision of questions of fact, unless the doctrine of 'colour' could be made applicable, was not a suitable instrument for dealing with cases turning on possibly complicated statements of account, nor in such cases could a single issue readily be reached by pleadings. Moreover all the parties to an account, and there might be several, could not be joined in one suit. The effect of these deficiencies was that by the end of the fifteenth century the fact that if in any case the taking of accounts was involved, the intervention of the Chancellor was

[1] See below, Ch. X, pp. 127–9.

invariably obtainable, and also, for much the same reasons, in cases concerning the administration of assets. Partners moreover could not hold one another to account, and it is hardly too much to say that partnership was ignored by the Common Law of this period. The Chancellor filled the gap.

Apart from the large number of cases which had failed at Common Law merely owing to verbal or formal errors, or slips in the pleadings, the most striking example of classes of cases falling under the second category, inadequacy of Common Law Rules and their limited application, is that of breach of contract. Until the middle of the fourteenth century the action of covenant was the only form of contract enforceable at Common Law. Like so many actions it originated in the land law, and was designed to protect leaseholders. By the end of the thirteenth century it had been extended to cover covenants not related to land, but the action could be brought only if there were a written undertaking, duly sealed. A sealed instrument was absolutely impregnable unless it could be met by another. It was conclusive, and no defence relying on extrinsic evidence was permissible.[1] Even if a man's seal had been stolen and fraudulently applied to a document of which he knew nothing, he was irrevocably bound. No allegation of fraud was accepted. About the middle of the fourteenth century a form of the action of trespass on the case was evolved (*assumpsit*) but it was treated as an action in tort and not in contract, and was available only where there had been definite misfeasance. The Common Law did not at the time envisage the desirability of enforcing agreements and accords as such. In 1436 it was at last held that breach of contract by non feasance was actionable, if actual loss had resulted, but this was not generally recognized till 1504. The rise of *assumpsit* did provide a common law remedy for the breach of parol contracts, but the impossibility of ordering specific performance still caused many applications to the Chancellor. Writs of 'assumpsit' had moreover to be drawn up with meticulous care, and the dialectical rigidity of the rules of pleading provided a multiplicity of potential pitfalls. What was wanted in the social and economic conditions of the fifteenth century was legal recogni-

---

[1] See *II Henry VI*, IV, ii.

Dick: The first thing we do, let's kill all the lawyers.

Cade: Nay, that I mean to do. Is not this a lamentable thing that of the skin of an innocent lamb should be made parchment? that parchment, being scribbled o'er, should undo a man? Some say the bee stings; but I say 'tis the bee's wax; for I did but seal once to a thing, and I was never mine own man since.

tion of simple business arrangements, not high technique and in-flexible rigidity. The Chancellor was entirely unmoved by the common law doctrines of the invincible superiority of a specialty,[1] or by the sacramental character of seals.

In addition to the classes of suit briefly sketched above, the Chancellor would often intervene on purely general grounds. The extreme poverty of the plaintiff was sometimes a ground for inter-ference in the dilatory and expensive 'course of the Courts', what-ever the subject matter of his grievance might be. He also felt the necessity for over-riding the survivals from antiquity, which still lived on in the Common Law. Law wager, or oath helping, could still be used by defendants (and was possible for centuries after-wards) in certain actions, notably Debt, Detinue and account.[2] The compurgators, or oath helpers, simply had to swear that they believed their principal's statement to be true, and the plaintiff then lost his case. The Chancellor would accept jurisdiction over cases where this method of defence had been adopted, merely because (like the Crown) he distrusted it.

It is clear, then, that up to the end of the fifteenth century, and indeed for the first few decades of the sixteenth, the operation of equity extended over a very wide field, the boundaries of which were not at all clearly defined. The business of life was becoming more varied and complex, trade and commerce were growing rapidly, particularly in the last quarter of the century, and required more efficient and speedier legal regulation than could be provided by "the intricate games of procedural chess"[3] whereby the judges of England were slowly endeavouring to adapt the rules of mediaeval land tenure to the needs of a changing world.

The Chancellor's Court was not tied down to the Law terms, but remained in session all the year round which was a boon to litigants. The procedure was simple and summary, as indeed it had to be if the Chancellor was to cope with the ever growing mass of judicial work which was heaped upon him. There was no avoid-able delay in securing the attendance of the defendant. Common Law process could be defeated by the defendant moving from place to place, or removing himself to a liberty, but the Chancellor's

[1] A specialty is a contract, obligation, or bond, expressed in an instrument under seal.

[2] It was not abolished till 1833.

[3] P. H. Winfield, *History of Conspiracy and Abuse of Legal Procedure*, Cambridge 1921.

'subpoena' was not restricted by county boundaries, or by privileged franchises. Nor was there a complicated system of pleading, or, indeed, any real system of pleading at all. "It was said by the Chancellor in the Chancery that a man shall not be prejudiced by mispleading, or by defects of form, but he shall be judged according to the truth of his case."[1] Even a glaring mistake or vital omission obviously due to simple-minded ignorance or negligence was over-looked. *Deus est procurator fatuorum* as Chancellor Stillington said in 1467.

The Chancellor, in brief, was guided by a simple principle of jurisprudence drawn from the Canon Law—the application to each individual case of the test of reason and conscience. Selden was hardly fair in his statement that the Chancellor's conscience must vary indeterminately with each individual Chancellor. Any ordinarily reasonable and intelligent person of experience can detect sharp practice when he sees it. Nor, unless he has been rigorously drilled and trained for years into unquestioning acceptance of the transcendant validity of rules and precedents, is he likely to allow the worse to be the better cause simply because of the skill and technical accuracy of its presentation.

The Chancellor also had advantages which the Common Law had not. He could, and always did, examine the defendant orally on oath. Then, as a rule, he delivered judgment. The plaintiff might be examined, also on oath, if his bill of complaint appeared to make this desirable, but, normally, that was all.[2] By the middle of the fifteenth century, however, the practice grew up of having the defendant's answer to the plaint recorded in writing by one of the Chancery clerks, before his sworn examination. It was then submitted to the Chancellor, along with the plaintiff's bill. This method seems to have developed from the occasional granting by the Chancellor of a writ (*dedimus potestatem*) to take the defendant's answer on commission.[3] The alteration, slight as it may seem, opened the way for the Common Lawyers, when their opportunity arose, to develop the written record of cases in equity, and marks the first beginnings of the change which was to make the Chancery more of a by-word for delay, expense, and uncertainty than the Courts of Common Law had ever been.

---

[1] *Year Book 9, Edward IV*. Quoted by Holdsworth, Vol. II, p. 596.
[2] *Select Cases in Chancery*, Selden Society, 1896, Introduction, p. XXVII.
[3] *Select Cases in Chancery*, Selden Society, 1896, Introduction, p. XXVII.

It is impossible to estimate the effectiveness of the Chancellor's equitable jurisdiction in this period. The weakness of the Central Government, and the frequently disturbed state of the country must often have made it impossible for his decrees to be translated into action.[1] Also the proportion of the bills presented upon which he did actually adjudicate is unknown. The Chancery was not a Court of Record, and at this time precedents were of no account, so remarkably few judgments (which were presumably given orally) have survived. All that can be said for certain is that people undoubtedly felt that there was at least a chance that they would obtain not merely an equitable judgment, but an actual remedy. Otherwise it is not possible to explain the vast and ever growing number of appeals to the Chancellor. There is certainly no doubt that the Chancellor could and did, by the issue of injunctions, prevent a very considerable number of false cases from ever coming before the courts. The Common Law judges were particularly hostile to this form of intervention.[2]

From the reign of Richard II onwards there were moreover frequent complaints in Parliament against the invasions of the field of Common Law by equity, which is an indication that the Chancellor's interference was at least moderately effective. Most of these originated in the Commons, and presumably were inspired by the Common Lawyers, who were a strong and influential element in the Lower House. Attempts were made as early as 1436 to extend the scope of the action of 'trespass on the case' in the form of 'assumpsit' to breach of contract by non-feasance, in an effort to appropriate or recover some at least of the jurisdiction acquired by the Chancellor. It seems certain that competition by the Chancery did act as a stimulant to the Common Lawyers to reform their time-honoured system, but the necessity of extracting 'the new corn from the old fields' made the progress of change and improvement inevitably slow.

In conclusion, when the 'New Monarchy' was established, the

[1] Jack Cade apparently had no more faith in the Chancellor than in the Common Law. In his proclamation as 'Captayn of ye Rebelles in Kent' he stated "Item, the law servyth of nowght ellys in these days, but for to do wrong, for nothyng is sped almost but false maters by coulour of the law for mede, drede, and favor, and so no remedy is had in ye Courte of Conscions in any wyse." *Three Fifteenth Century Chronicles,* ed. Kingsford, Camden Society, 1880, p. 96.

[2] A case is recorded in *Year Book 22 Edward IV,* of the judges advising a plaintiff to proceed in spite of the Chancellor's injunction, and promising to release him by writ of Habeas Corpus, if he were imprisoned as a result of his disobedience.

Chancellor, unhampered by precedents and technicalities of any kind, might be in a position to provide swift, cheap and equitable justice to those who could reach him. Blackstone, who was naturally hostile to equity, sums up the position as follows—"No regular judicial system at that time prevailed in the Court; but the suitor, when he thought himself aggrieved, found a desultory and uncertain remedy, according to the private opinion of the Chancellor, who was generally an ecclesiastic, and sometimes (though rarely) a statesman."[1]

[1] Blackstone, *Commentaries*, iii, 53.

CHAPTER VI

THE CRIMINAL LAW

LIKE the Civil Law, the Criminal Law of England was based upon the innovations of the Angevin Kings. Henry II instituted the jury of indictment. If the jurors, fairly substantial freeholders of the hundred, stated on oath that a person was suspected of murder or felony, he was sent to the ordeal. After the fourth Lateran Council of 1215, when Pope Innocent III forbade the clergy to assist, the ordeal disappeared from legal procedure, except the Ordeal by Battle, for which clerical intervention was unnecessary, and in trials for witchcraft. Something had to be found to take its place. The answer was again a jury of neighbours—at first consisting wholly or mainly of the indicting jury, later, in order to be fair to the accused, of different jurors—the petty jury.

Maitland considered that the popularity of jury trial was doubtful. He admits indeed that it was only the uniquely powerful Central Government of the Angevin Kings that made the system applicable to criminal proceedings,[1] and this of course includes, though he does not say so, its use to decide questions of fact in civil cases in which influential people were interested.[2] But from the time of Edward II the Central Government had not been at all powerful, and from the latter part of the fourteenth century till 1471 it was usually deplorably weak, and at times existed only in name. The legal profession had, however, come to regard jury trial as an integral part of the Common Law, and in the middle of the fifteenth century, the Lancastrian Chief Justice, Sir John Fortescue, in a work which illustrates most admirably the mental attitude of the Common Lawyers of his day (and after), described the system as faultless, and that at a time when a wholly intolerable proportion of false verdicts had made a mockery of justice. The facts did not concern him, though no one can have been more familiar with them than he. They

[1] "The Common Law was essentially the law of property; its courts, procedure and practitioners were all organised for the conduct of property legislation. Police regulations had to be treated in.terms of debt and detinue." Plucknett, *Some Proposed Legislation of Henry VIII*, R.H.S.T., 4th Series, Vol. 19, 1936.

[2] Pollock and Maitland, op. cit., Vol. II, p. 631.

were not deducible from the purely theoretical aspect of the institution. Juries, he must have known, could be and were bought or intimidated, and sheriffs and undersheriffs bribed or influenced to select a panel which would bring in the desired verdict. Yet he could write that jury trial was unsurpassed, and indeed unsurpassable, as a method of eliciting the truth, and less exposed than any other to the dangers of subornation.[1] He was determined to denigrate the law of Rome, which knew not the jury, but relied much more on witnesses than did the Common Law. Jurors were half witnesses themselves, half judges of fact. They were chosen from the neighbourhood because it was expected that they would know at least something of the facts or probabilities of the case. The production of evidence to which they might listen was not essential. They might be called upon to pronounce a verdict without having heard any evidence at all. How much better was it, said Fortescue, to depend on the findings of such jurors, respectable freemen, men with a stake in the country, and with reputations to lose, chosen moreover by a high officer of honour and impartiality, than on unknown persons, brought to court by the parties, who might well be hired scoundrels or worthless vagrants? Moreover if witnesses were produced, the jurors would know exactly the sort of people they were and what degree of reliance was to be placed on their statements. Finally, in the unlikely event of a jury of neighbours bringing in a false verdict, the injured party might sue out a writ of attaint against them. The jury of attaint numbered twenty-four instead of twelve, and had a higher property qualification. If they found the original verdict to have been false, the forsworn jurors were liable to imprisonment and confiscation of all their goods. Further, their houses would be destroyed, their pastures ploughed, their woods cut down, and they themselves declared to be permanently infamous and incapable of testifying. Surely this was a sufficient safeguard. It is true that the jurors were normally respectable freeholders, in at least a moderately good position. But even if they were honest men, what could ordinary small farmers do in a countryside dominated by robber barons and their jackals? As for the writ of attaint, it did exist, but it is doubtful whether Fortescue could have quoted a single instance of its tremendous sanctions having been applied in his time. Still it was available, and theoretically should have proved effective.

[1] Sir John Fortescue, op. cit., XXVI, p. 59 and XXIX, p. 77.

Suspected criminals must often have been convicted simply on their local reputations. The odds indeed were in one way heavily weighted against the man who had no efficient protector. He could not give evidence himself, nor could he summon witnesses, nor had he the assistance of Counsel. On the other hand, the complete verbal accuracy required in indictments was in his favour. The judges treated the indictment as they treated all written records, and the formalism of criminal procedure equalled that of the civil side, and long outlasted it, in spite of the fact that the administration of criminal justice was mainly carried on by non-professionals. A legal education was not thought to be necessary for a criminal judge. The members of commissions of Gaol Delivery were by no means exclusively trained lawyers, nor were the majority of the Justices of the Peace, who became responsible for doing most of the ordinary criminal work of the country. The procedure did not lend itself to dialectical skill. Precedents were normally of no account, and pleadings did not exist. The indictment on the other hand was a record on which the Common Law judges could exercise their legal learning. The requirements for a valid indictment at this time were that the name and address of the accused, and the place where he committed the crime must be accurately stated. Any error meant the quashing of the indictment. The date also must be precisely given. If, for example, a man were accused of an offence committed on the day of the Feast of S. Peter, the indictment was held to be defective, as there were two Feasts of S. Peter in the year. The name of the victim also must be stated correctly, if it were known. If it were not, he was to be described as 'quidam ignotus'. The actual crime also had to be precisely described in detail. Finally the conclusion of the indictment must be that the offence was committed 'contra pacem domini regis'. If the words 'domini regis' were omitted, the indictment was liable to be quashed.[1]

Even if the indictment was held to be insufficient after the accused had been found guilty, he was discharged. None of the statutes of Jeofail, which allowed of the correction of various formal errors in the record of a civil case, applied to indictments, which invariably had to be technically perfect. These rules appear to be survivals from the time before the introduction of indictments, when 'appeals', that is, oral complaints by the injured person or his representatives, were dismissed *in limine* if a verbal slip was made. They were justi-

[1] Holdsworth, *History of English Law*, Vol. II, p. 617.

fied by the unanswerable argument that the utmost degree of certainty was necessary in capital cases. It is however to be observed that certainty of proof by evidence of the actual facts was not required, but merely complete verbal accuracy in the formal statement of the accusation, which might itself be entirely unfounded.

There can be no doubt that many criminals escaped owing to these 'unseemly niceties' as Chief Justice Hale called them. Moreover it was only a small proportion who ever came to trial at all. Powers of arrest were extremely limited, and continued to be so throughout the sixteenth century and far into the seventeenth. As late as 1523 it was held that a Justice of the Peace could not issue a warrant of arrest against a person who had not been indicted unless he himself suspected him (Year Book 14, Henry VIII). Even those who had been duly indicted usually had opportunities to escape, and it seems that a great number did.

Further, the otherwise unprotected blackguard had the chance of taking sanctuary. If he could get into any parish church or churchyard he was safe from the gallows. For up to forty days he could stay there. At any time during that period he could confess his crime before the coroner and abjure the realm, after which he was dispatched to the nearest seaport. Even if he did not escape *en route* from the village constable who accompanied him he could hope to return undetected from exile. But churches were not the only sanctuaries. There were whole tracts of country which were, the Palatinates, the Marcher Lordships of Wales, the Archbishop of York's liberties of Beverley, Ripon, and Hexham, the liberty of Tynemouth, the liberty of the Abbot of S. Mary's, York, the great lay liberties of Redesdale and Tynedale, and many smaller ones all over the country. One there was in Westminster—the Abbey precincts—and one in London—S. Martin's le Grand—where the sanctuary men were sufficiently numerous to cause serious disorder in Henry VII's time. To none of these sanctuaries did the forty day limit apply. If a criminal escaped to one of them he was safe so long as he stayed there. Henry VIII abolished all sanctuaries except parish churches and churchyards, but there the privilege lingered on till 1623.[1]

Benefit of clergy was another abuse tending to encourage lawlessness, which, so far from being curtailed, was eventually extended to cover not only those actually in orders, including minor orders,

---

[1] See I. D. Thornely, *Sanctuary*, Tudor Studies, ed. Seton Watson.

but all who could read. The author of the Italian Relation of England (*c.* 1500)[1] was astonished at the privilege of sanctuary, and also at Benefit of Clergy, and attributed to them the excessively high level of crime in England.

Quite apart from the complete breakdown of the system of indictment and trial by jury owing to the disturbed condition of the country, it cannot be said that the criminal law at the end of the fifteenth century was well adapted to the maintenance of order.

[1] *An Italian Relation of England*, Camden Society, 1847, pp. 34–6.

CHAPTER VII

THE RESTORATION OF ORDER
(I) THE YORKISTS

LAW and order do not necessarily go together, though the words are often used in conjunction. There was plenty of law in fifteenth-century England. Throughout its worst days the Courts of Westminster continued to sit, apparently unperturbed, and had plenty of business.[1] "The forms of law and physical violence had come to be merely alternative instruments to be used as seemed most expedient."[2] This was the reason why a knowledge of the law was at this period so widely diffused. The Paston Letters afford ample evidence that every man who had property to protect was perfectly well versed in the ordinary forms of legal process.[3] It was as necessary for self protection (or for aggression) as a knowledge of the use of warlike weapons. "The law was no longer a shield for the weak and oppressed—rather it was a sword for the inscrupulous. Men learned its rules as they learned the rules of sword play."

It seems possible that the economic recession of the fifteenth century, which accentuated the poverty of the Crown, was also partly at least responsible for the restlessness of the upper classes, and the turning of a considerable proportion of them to the methods of the gangster. A slump appears to have begun late in the fourteenth century (the aftermath of the Black Death may have had something to do with it) and to have lasted until the last quarter of the fifteenth. Prices had fallen; wages had risen, and the landlords were the class which suffered, just as they did in the great price rise of Edward VI's time. It was not only the cessation of the Hundred Years War and the return to England of large numbers of indentured soldiery which encouraged the aristocracy and gentry to remove their poorer neighbours' landmarks.

[1] M. Hastings, *The Court of Common Pleas in 15th Century England*, Cornell University Press, 1947, pp. 7 et seq.
[2] Holdsworth, *History of English Law*, Vol. II, p. 416.
[3] *Paston Letters*, ed. Gairdner, Vol I, pp. 118–19.

The upper classes had long recognized that the Common Law suited them well. The dependence of the system upon juries and subordinate officials was highly advantageous to the wealthy and unscrupulous. They were in a position to influence sheriffs and deputy sheriffs, and overawe or bribe jurors, and also, when necessary, to fee skilled lawyers. They frequently had close relations with the leaders of the legal profession, which was extremely well represented in Parliament, and had been ever since the time of Edward III. Certainly thirty-seven, and possibly forty-three lawyers sat in Henry VI's first Parliament, out of a total membership of two hundred and sixty-two, and of these no less than twenty were knights of the shire. A few of them were in the service of the Crown, but the great majority were in that of one or more of the great baronial houses.[1] It appears that the pattern of the 1422 Lower House did not vary very much throughout the fifteenth century, nor indeed for long after, and it seems certain that at no time during the whole of our period did either of the Houses cause the Common Lawyers to feel the slightest apprehension, whatever the feeling might be against them in the country at large.

It cannot be too strongly emphasized that throughout this period, and indeed for long after it, the upper grades of the legal profession, those who were, or had been, members of an Inn of Court, were as a general rule practically indistinguishable in education and in social status from prosperous country gentry, to which class most of them belonged. In addition to being the nursery of professional advocates, the Inns of Court made provision for the teaching of polite accomplishments, such as dancing and fencing, and their revels and masques were famous. They constituted in some sort a gentleman's university. A high proportion of those who owned landed property spent some time in an Inn of Court, partly to enjoy themselves, and partly to learn the rudiments of the Common Law. Those who adopted advocacy as a profession always tended to be of the same class, though Fortescue perhaps exaggerates slightly when he says that there was hardly anyone learned in the law who was not of noble descent.[2] Life at an Inn of Court was expensive, and there were no exhibitions, as there were to the universities, to open a legal career to the poor man. The intimate and closely knit alliance

---

[1] J. S. Roskell, *The Commons in the Parliament of 1422*, Manchester University Press, 1954, pp. 66–8.

[2] Sir John Fortescue, *De Laudibus Legum Angliae*, ed. S. B. Chrimes, XLIX, p. 117.

E

between the upper classes and the Common Lawyers, added to
the unique constitutional significance of Common Law principle,
made anything like root and branch reform utterly impracticable.

It is true that when the dynastic quarrel was superadded to the
inefficiency bred of greed and gangsterism, the stranglehold of the
oligarchs on the monarchy was relaxed. During the Wars of the
Roses the baronage exhausted itself, and what may properly be
called the crowning mercy of Tewkesbury gave Edward IV and his
successors a free hand in choosing their advisers and assistants.
There were no over-riding individual personal interests or claims to
be considered, and until the collapse of the monarchy in 1641, the King
could pursue his policies unhampered by the presence of hostile or
potentially hostile elements within the governing circle. His predecessors had been unable to rely on their Council for co-operation
in the suppression of disorders, because it came to be dominated by
the very people responsible for the violent outrages and abuse of legal
process characteristic of the period. From the time of Richard II it
seems to have been most reluctant to take effective action against
nobles, gentry, or their retainers.[1] No support was to be looked for
from Parliament, which did not represent the mass of the people, but
which did represent their rulers and leaders. Palgrave has illustrated
from the Rolls of Parliament the ceaseless oposition of the Commons
to conciliar interference with the Courts of Common Law, both
in civil and criminal cases. It was not only the few great territorial
magnates with their armies of retainers with whom the King had
to reckon. Many members of the Lower House were little less
powerful than the lesser nobility, and they and many of their
fellows had, generally speaking, a community of interest with
the magnates— the hope of gain.[2] Few of the Knights of the Shire,
who counted for far more than the more numerous burgesses,
had neither direct interest nor kinship with the Parliamentary
aristocracy.

---

[1] See *Case of Esturmy* v. *the Earl of Devonshire*, late in the reign of Richard II.
A servant of a retainer of the Earl had committed a murder, but owing to the Earl's
protection all efforts to arrest him failed. Eventually the Earl surrendered, and on the
recommendation of the Council was pardoned, not only for this particular act of
maintenance, but for every crime previously committed by him. A few years later,
the actual murderer—who had never been arrested—was also pardoned. *Select
Cases in the King's Council*, Selden Society, Baldwin and Leadam.

[2] J. S. Roskell, op. cit., pp. 46-7.

The last resort was the Court of Chancery. In addition to taking over the work of the King and Council in the field of Civil Law, the task of checking the outrages of the overmighty subject was delegated to him. The opposition to his intervention had not been strenuous. He was merely assisting the King to discharge the obligations of his Coronation Oath, and no one could openly object to that, provided that he did not overstep the mark. The Common Lawyers did begin to show signs of restiveness, but they had to recognize that in some classes of case the Common Law as it stood could provide no remedy whatever, and also that the King was bound to do equitable justice in hard cases. The great nobles and their followers were not seriously inconvenienced, as the Chancellor's proceedings against their doings can in the conditions of the time rarely have been decisively effective. He had, however, at least shown the way. After 1471 there was no longer any need to rely upon a single over-burdened ecclesiastic, and the obvious course was for the King in Council to resume, to the extent thought necessary and possible, the judicial powers which had been delegated nearly three hundred years before, and deal with the main sources of disorder and discontent unhampered by abstruse technicalities, intricate rules, archaic formalism, and above all by dependence on the broken reed of the jury system.

But the King had by no means a clean slate. A pencil he now possessed, but no sponge. The forces of misrule had received a severe check, but they were by no means crippled. Parliament had for long always been desirous of leaving the protection of both person and property to the Common Law, and far from tending to remit jurisdiction over new or exceptionally troublesome classes of cases to the central authority, tended rather to restrict its judicial competence. The King had never abandoned his right to reserve whatever cases he pleased, either civil or criminal, for consideration or decision by himself in Council, but the statutory restrictions on conciliar jurisdiction were drastic. The Council was debarred by the statute 25 Edward III from entertaining any case touching free-hold or a franchise. The Commons had attempted to include matters of life and limb in the disqualification. The King declined to agree to this, but conviction for treason or felony involved the forfeiture of all property, and hence it came to be universally considered that the Council could in no circumstances award the death penalty. The King in practice accepted this restriction on his residuary powers, serious though it was. Edward IV had no reason to suppose that the parliamentary attitude of hostility to conciliar jurisdiction was definitely relaxed. Moreover, though he could now choose his own assistants, he had no other advantage, and could not hope to break through the 'Regimen regale et politicum'.

Caution was obviously necessary even to the victor of Tewkesbury. Also, although he was capable of energetic action on occasion, he was lazy and self-indulgent, and he seems to have had no minister of outstanding capacity. All that he felt able to do was unobtrusively to revive the judicial activity of the Council. For a century or so the dispatch of a Commission of Oyer et Terminer had usually been thought preferable to a trial by Council, even in cases of exaggerated outrage. Since the close of the thirteenth century hardly a hundred cases appear actually to have been heard from beginning to end,[1] and a large proportion of them was taken up because they affected the King's personal interests, or the misdoings of his servants. During the Lancastrian period nothing effective could be done to check the disorderliness of the highly placed, and during the Wars of the Roses the Council functioned only intermittently. Even after the triumph of the Yorkists direct and stringent measures were rarely taken, and then only in individual cases, to deal with the long-standing evils of livery and maintenance, champerty and embracery, but a definite beginning was made,[2] which paved the way for the more vigorous action of Henry VII, and the much more vigorous action of Cardinal Wolsey. However, before the end of Edward's reign the Council did regularly hear cases in the Star Chamber at Westminster, which had been its headquarters since the time of Edward III, and it continued to do so throughout the brief reign of Richard III. It does not seem ever to have started proceedings on behalf of the Crown on its own initiative, but to have confined itself to bills between party and party.[3] Special attention appears to have been paid by the Council to the grievances of the poor, and the origins of what became the specialized Court of Requests are to be looked for in the reign of Richard III, if not in that of Edward IV.

The procedure employed by the Council was a simplified variant

[1] *Select Cases in the King's Council*, Selden Society, Baldwin and Leadam.
[2] *Select Cases in the King's Council*, Selden Society, Baldwin and Leadam.
[3] S. B. Chrimes, *An introduction to the Administrative History of Mediaeval England*, Oxford 1952, p. 260.

of that in use in Courts of Civil or Canon Law, and its adoption may be ascribed to the ecclesiastical element, and especially to the Chancellor. Proceedings were started by a petition, or bill, which was not a formal document. The plaintiff had merely to state his grievance. Summons was sometimes by a letter missive, but usually by writ of privy seal, in which, unlike the normal writ ordinarily issued, details of the accusation were not entered. The suspect was simply bidden to appear before the Council on a fixed date to answer 'concerning certain matters'. He might not, and probably often did not, know which particular outrage had come to notice, nor the name of his accuser, so was unable to take steps to see that the matter went no further. These writs of privy seal were backed by a 'subpoena', imposing a penalty, usually of from twenty to two hundred pounds, for failure to appear. This was an effective means of securing attendance, and was much disliked by Parliament. The King never agreed to abandon the issue of these writs, and in 1453 Parliament was persuaded by the shock of Jack Cade's rebellion in 1450 to give statutory authority for their issue, in riot cases only, and for a period of seven years. The Yorkists appear to have paid no attention to either limitation.

The defendant on appearance was confronted with the charges. If his answers were unsatisfactory he was examined on oath, which was the regular method of the Civil and Canon Laws. When there were several accused, each was examined separately, and the admissions of one were used against the others.

Juries were never used, save occasionally to give an answer to a question of fact in a civil case, and witnesses at this time were not usually required. Civil and Canon Law procedure could be extremely dilatory, and so could the conciliar variant of it, as exemplified in the proceedings of the Court of Admiralty, but the proceedings of the King's Council were normally expeditious, both in criminal and civil cases.

The same procedure was employed by the Council of Wales and the Marches, which seems to have been established at least on a temporary basis in order to cope with the highly anarchical condition of that country, and also by the Council of the North, which began to be effective in 1472, and was re-organized, under the King's Lieutenant, as a court of justice possessing both civil and criminal jurisdiction in 1484. There was no opposition at the time to this very considerable extension of the sphere of prerogative justice. It

was presumably recognized by all except the local grandees that
provision ought to be made for the administration of justice on the
spot in these remote and barbarous areas. The lawyers too were not
interested, as very little business was forthcoming either from Wales
or the North.

CHAPTER VIII

THE RESTORATION OF ORDER
(II) HENRY VII

HENRY VII's achievement was to underline the supremacy of the executive government, which had been restored by the Yorkists, over both the financial and judicial hierarchies, freed as far as possible from the maze of technicalities and conventions with which both these bodies had surrounded themselves. Unfortunately, though perhaps inevitably, Henry VII looked to the law and lawyers as the fittest instruments for building up his financial position.

There was a long series of precedents. The Kings seem, when they were strong enough, always to have regarded the extension of the profits of justice as the most practical means of enabling themselves to rule as national monarchs with ambitious foreign policies on what was, apart from customs duties, a largely feudal income. The desire to increase his scanty resources was probably one of the reasons, if not the main reason, why Henry II determined to centralize the administration of justice. Allusion has already been made to Edward I's attitude.[1] His conduct after the great judicial scandal of 1289, as a result of which a number of judges were imprisoned and fined for gross corruption, perhaps also deserves notice. He was heavily in debt to Italian money lenders, and seems to have decided to make the judges and other officials disgorge at least a proportion of their ill-gotten gains for his benefit rather than punish them as they deserved. R. de Hengham, Chief Justice of the King's Bench was fined seven thousand marks, but in 1301 was appointed to the more lucrative office of Chief Justice of the Common Pleas. The Chronicler, Bartholomew de Cotton, remarks—"All the judges made fine with the King . . . and so, by the intervention of the mammon of unrighteousness, peace was re-established between them and the King."[2] Holdsworth draws a parallel between Edward's abuse of the law to supply his necessities, with the aid of

[1] P. 28.
[2] T. F. Tout and Hilda Johnstone, *State Trials of Edward I*, Camden Society, 1906.

Stratton and the judges, and that of Henry VII.[1] Edward III also relied upon the profits of justice to supplement the loans of foreign bankers in the provision of the sinews of war. The campaigns of Crecy and Poitiers were financed largely from the takings of the Courts.[2] Henry VII, though he made something out of the suppression of crime, made much more by the enforcement of economic regulations, and also by the revival of obsolete statutes. He also relied on the use of legal process for the resuscitation of his feudal dues, and his Councillors Empson and Dudley owe their notoriety to their often unscrupulous rigour in the prosecution of his claims. Bacon wrote "He kept a strait hand on his nobility, and chose rather to advance clergymen and lawyers, which were more subservient to him, but had less interest in the people."[3]

Henry's motto might well have been "First things first", and no doubt the rehabilitation of the Crown's finances was an indispensable preliminary to the thorough restoration of order. He did not however abandon the work begun by his Yorkist predecessors, and he did make some progress in the suppression of crime and intimidation. Also, again like the Yorkists, he showed himself to be determined, in the face of considerable opposition, that common justice in civil matters should not be out of the reach of the common man, and here too he achieved a measure of success. But he was the last man to kill a goose that laid golden eggs, and he relied very largely on Common Lawyers to loosen the purse strings of his subjects. Possibly, indeed probably, the idea of radically changing what was already an ancient system, difficult to accomplish without highly skilled aid, and bound to encounter strenuous opposition from the classes on whom he depended for support, never entered his head. A compromise was, perhaps unconsciously, accepted which endured to the end of the period, whereby the operation of the Common Law was superseded in certain spheres, where its continued supremacy would make grievous discontent and possibly disaster inevitable, and allowed to continue its ancient reign, undisturbed and unreformed, in the remainder.

It has been said that Henry VII was not in any way an innovator, but that he developed existing institutions and made them work

---

[1] Holdsworth, *History of English Law*, Vol. IV, p. 26.

[2] B. Putnam, *The Place in Legal History of Sir William Shareshulle*, Cambridge Studies in Legal History, p. 78.

[3] F. Bacon, *History of Henry VII*, *Works*, ed. Ellis and Spedding, Vol. VI, p. 242.

efficiently. This is not true of his organization of the Council. He had, it is true, like his predecessors, a very large number of councillors. The names of one hundred and seventy-two are known, of whom one hundred and forty-six were present at one or more of the forty-six lists of attendances at meetings which have survived from his time.[1] Some he used a great deal, others hardly at all. The Privy Council is usually said not to have been established till 1540. It is true that it was not officially recognized till that date, at earliest, and that it did not acquire a seal of its own till the time of Philip and Mary, but every King did have in fact a Privy Council, in the sense that he used and trusted some councillors, usually very few, more than he did the others. Sir Reginald Bray, Sir Thomas Lovell, and Savage, Bishop of Rochester, were Henry's most trusted advisers, and Giles Daubeney, his Chamberlain, and Robert Willoughby de Broke, were also mentioned by Polydore Vergil as members of the inner ring. Apart from these, he may be considered as having a pool of councillors, into which he could dip for any purpose for which they seemed suitable.

Where he innovated was to create what amounted to standing Committees of Council, not chosen haphazardly, but consisting always of more or less the same members, to deal mainly with judicial work.

The existence of one of these—the King's Council learned in the Law—'consilium domini regis in lege eruditum'—has only recently become known, some of its records having been discovered among those of the Duchy of Lancaster.[2] The presiding officer was Sir Reginald Bray, who was perhaps more in Henry's confidence than anyone else. The other members were Roger Leyburne, Bishop of Carlisle, who was Bray's assistant as principal Crown auditor; Robert Sherbourne, Bishop of S. David's; Thomas Lucas, the King's Solicitor; Sir James Hobart, Attorney-General; Sir Humphrey Comingsby, Sir Robert Brudenel, and Richard Hesketh, Judges; William Smith, William Mordaunt (King's Attorney), Edmund Dudley and Sir Richard Empson. The King was never present. With the exceptions of Bray and the bishops, all were experienced lawyers. The procedure used, however, was that of the Council. The main reason for the employment of Common Lawyers—

[1] A. Conway, *Henry VII's Relations with Scotland and Ireland,* Cambridge, Appendix XLI, pp. 229–30.
[2] Henry VII's Council Learned in the Law, R. Somerville, *E.H.R.,* LVI.

(civilians and canonists—*in legibus eruditi*—were to be had in plenty) —was presumably that an accurate knowledge of the manifold intricacies of the land law would be invaluable in the task of reviving and recovering the King's feudal dues. But the Council learned in the law was not limited to financial exactions. It was concerned with both Henry's main preoccupations, the rehabilitation of the financial position of the Crown, and also the suppression of the typical contemporary outrages and abuse of legal process. The classes of case that came before this body included riots; misdemeanours of sheriffs and juries; false returns; coining (a class of crime in which Council was always particularly interested); the exporting of wool without licence, the shearing of worsted, forest offences, giving land in mortmain; and—probably the most numerous—failure to pay the King his dues as chief feudal lord, and failure to take up the order of knighthood. In the majority of cases before this body, proceedings were not initiated by bill, but directly by the Crown. Some cases between party and party were however heard, most of which concerned property. It is not known when this sub-committee came into existence. The records date from 1504 to 1509. It ceased to function on the accession of Henry VIII, presumably because the 'Council learned' was tarred as a whole with the same brush as two of its most prominent members, the ill-fated Dudley and Empson. Also thanks to the good management of Henry and his chosen helpers, there was no longer any pressing need for 'fiscales judices', and the work which they had done in the suppression of disorder was resumed by the undifferentiated Council, usually presided over by the Chancellor, and sitting in the Star Chamber at Westminster. Some cases were dealt with in this way throughout Henry's reign, but not very many. For the great days of the Council sitting as a judicial tribunal in the Star Chamber one must wait till the ascendancy of Wolsey.

Another small Committee of Council was set up (though only on paper) in 1487, by what has been wrongly known as "the Star Chamber Act". This little Act, strangely termed by Professor Baldwin 'this great statute' gave statutory authority to the central core of the Council to try certain classes of offence, and though it appears never to have been used, has given so much trouble to constitutional lawyers and historians, and has been responsible for so many curious theories that it seems necessary to examine it in some detail.

It laid down that the Chancellor, Treasurer, and Keeper of the

Privy Seal, or two of them, with a bishop and a temporal lord of the Council, and the two Chief Justices, or two other judges in their absence, were empowered to try eight named offences—livery, maintenance, indenture of retainers, corrupt appointment of jurors by sheriffs, embracery, corruption by jurors, riot and unlawful assembly—by conciliar procedure, and to punish those found guilty "in like manner and form as they shall and ought to be punished if they were thereof convict after the due order of the law."[1]

Some time about the middle of the sixteenth century a clerk who had presumably by chance lighted on this forgotten statute entered in the margin the fatal words "Pro Camera Stellata". Occasional jurisdiction by the Council was probably as old as the monarchy itself, but, as has been mentioned above, it had actually tried very few cases during the past two hundred years or more. But by the time the Clerk made his entry, and for three or four decades previously, what looked exactly like a new Court of Criminal Justice had appeared, attended by the Chief Justices or other judges, sitting regularly during term-time like the Courts of Common Law, and deciding very large numbers of cases, many of them triable at Common Law. It was, at the time of the marginal entry, still to a considerable extent occupied with the classes of offence enumerated in the Act—though by no means entirely. It was surely reasonable to suppose, in view of the statutes of the past two centuries, that Parliament must have agreed to the regularized wholesale assumption of judicial authority by the Council. The unknown clerk doubtless thought that he had found the Act creating what was even then (and still is) popularly known as the 'Court' of Star Chamber.

Sir Thomas Smith, who wrote his *De Republica Anglorum* about 1565 does not mention the Act of 1487 at all, but attributes the increase of conciliar cases to Wolsey, in which he seems to have been quite right.[2] The person who first drew public attention to the Act seems to have been the great Common Lawyer Edmund Plowden who some time fairly late in the reign of Elizabeth I raised an objection to the trial of a case in the Star Chamber on the ground that the offence with which the accused was charged was not one of those enumerated in the Statute. He apparently believed, or at least affected on this occasion to believe, that the judicial powers of the Council derived their legal authority from the Act of 1487. Sir

[1] J. R. Tanner, *Tudor Constitutional Documents 1485-1603*, pp. 258-9.
[2] Sir Thomas Smith, *De Republica Anglorum*, ed. L. Alston, 1906, Book III, IV.

Edward Coke, though he realized that the jurisdiction of the Council was far more ancient than the Act of 3 Henry VII, was nevertheless much puzzled by the fact that the limitations therein laid down both as to the classes of offence triable, and as to the personnel entitled to hear them, were not observed in practice. The only reason he could find for the failure to follow its provisions was "that the Act of 3 Henry VII being in the affirmative, is not in some things pursued", and that therefore the doings of the Council in the Star Chamber "must have warrant from the Ancient Court".[1] Coke held that statutes in the affirmative—i.e. those giving a positive command—did not necessarily alter the previous position, but that statutes giving a negative command were to be interpreted as declaring new law, and must be obeyed absolutely. This distinction is not found earlier than the reign of Edward IV, but it is interesting to compare it with Bishop Pecock's doctrine (c. 1395–1460) that the negative commands of God were absolutely binding, whereas His affirmative injunctions were binding only relatively. For example the commandment "Honour thy father and thy mother" must be to some extent flexible. On the other hand, the Commandment "Thou shalt not steal" is completely rigid.

Bacon (1621) thought that "the authority of the Star Chamber which before subsisted by the ancient common laws of the realm" (he is here using the word 'common law' as meaning what Pym called "the ancient and fundamental law, issuing from the first frame and constitution of the kingdom") was confirmed in certain cases by Act of Parliament. He recognized that 3 Henry VII C. 1 did not create the jurisdiction concerned, but believed that it gave statutory authority to its exercise in some classes of offence.[2]

Modern historians have propounded other theories, the most remarkable of which is that put forward by the late Professor Pollard. He thought that the Act should be interpreted in the light of another item in the same statute of 1487, 3 Henry VII C. 14, which gave the great household officials (Steward, Treasurer and Comptroller) power to try members of the Royal Household under the estate of lords, for conspiring against the King, a lord, or a King's Councillor and condemn them for felony.[3] He apparently regarded 3 Henry VII C. 1 as instituting a powerful Committee of Council

---

[1] Sir Edward Coke, *Fourth Institute*, V.
[2] F. Bacon, *Maxims of the Law*, Works, ed. Spedding, VII, p. 379.
[3] A. F. Pollard, The Star Chamber, *E.H.R.*, 1922.

for dealing with riots, maintenance etc. for which the King's own household were responsible, and he explains the absence of records as due to the King's reluctance to publicize the washing of the dirty linen of his own establishment. There seems to be no evidence, direct or indirect, to support this theory. The Act was, *inter alia*, aimed at the 'untrue demeanings of sheriffs' and the 'taking of money by juries'. Also where was there the need to obtain statutory permission for the trial of members of the Royal Household, when they could perfectly well have been tried by the Council without it?

Mr. W. F. Baildon, who seems to be followed by Professor Baldwin, thinks that the Act was passed to delimit the spheres of Council and Chancery.[1] Chancery was to be limited to equitable civil jurisdiction, while the Council was left to deal with crime.

Mr. I. S. Leadam, who is followed by Dr. Pickthorn, believed that the primary object of the Act was to obtain parliamentary sanction for the exercise of the traditional procedure of the Council, especially for the use of writs of privy seal, statutory sanction for which had long expired.[2] But it seems improbable that Henry, who, from the wording of the Act, obviously initiated the measure, would have gone to the trouble of doing so merely to receive fresh sanction to the time-honoured practice of summons by writ of privy seal especially in view of the fact that there had been no complaints about the use of it for many years. Also it is not clear, if he did think it necessary to obtain a renewed sanction, why he should have deliberately restricted its application to a small body headed by three great officers of State, the busiest men in England, who could seldom be present together to try more than an occasional case of overwhelmingly 'enormous' nature. Also, though arguments were frequently put forward in the time of Henry VII and Henry VIII, Edward VI, and Philip and Mary that a case ought to be remitted to the Common Law Courts as being there determinable, the Act of 1487 and its highly restrictive provisions were never mentioned as a bar to conciliar proceedings until well on in the reign of Elizabeth I, and then not because of the use of writs of privy seal. In fact, as Dicey saw, Henry VII's statute bore no relation whatever to ordinary conciliar jurisdiction in the Star Chamber.[3] In the last sentence of the

---

[1] *Select Cases in Chancery*, ed. W. P. Baildon, Selden Society, 1896, Introduction, pp. 20–1.

[2] *Select Cases in the Star Chamber*, Vol. I, Selden Society, Introduction; and K. W. M. Pickthorn, *Early Tudor Government*, Vol. I (Henry VII).

[3] A. V. Dicey, *Privy Council*.

Act lies the key to the mystery. Hallam thought that the Act must have been used, as it was amended in 1529, when the President of the Council was added to the membership laid down in 1487. His conclusion does not, however, necessarily follow. The mere existence of the Act had its uses—'in terrorem'. The Council, by long established convention, could not touch life, or limb, and was forbidden by statute to touch freehold. What the Act of 1487 did was to give authority to a special conciliar tribunal when constituted in a particular way, to break both statute and convention and inflict statutory or common law penalties on certain classes of offenders 'in like manner and form as they should and ought to be punished if they were thereof convict after the due order of the law". This interpretation explains all the difficulties. None but the greatest officers of State, helped by the Chief Justices, were to be given these terrifying powers, and it was probably not envisaged that they would often be employed, but the fact that a reserve weapon of such potency existed might well have been expected to serve as a deterrent.[1]

It has been thought desirable to deal moderately fully with the story of 3 Henry VII C. 1 because, apart from the trouble which its interpretation has caused, in spite of the weight of evidence against the theory first put forward by Plowden, it was that theory which prevailed in 1641, when the 'Court of Star Chamber' was abolished for the ostensible reason that it was illegal and usurpatory, in that it had failed to observe the limitations laid down in the Act of 1487.

[1] R. R. Steele, *Catalogue of Tudor and Stuart Proclamations* (*Bibliotheca Lindesiana*), Vol. I, Introduction, p. LXXVI.

It is perhaps worth while to point out that Henry VIII obtained in the Statute of Proclamations (1539) statutory authority for certain named members of his Council to inflict the terrible punishment for treason on such as "obstinately, willingly, or contemptuously avoid and depart out of the realm" in order to escape the necessity of answering for offences under the Act. The Statute of Proclamations gave Henry's ordinances the force of law, and has been described as marking "the highest point of legal authority ever reached by the Crown". But no proclamation was made under it which could not have been made before. Why then was it passed? It may be that Henry, who in spite of his boundless egotism and pertinacious determination to get his own way, always liked to have cover if he thought that his actions might cause serious resentment, decided that parliamentary authority would be a desirable safeguard against troubles likely to arise from filling up the gaps in the Act of Settlement, which was the task immediately in view. Also it is certain that power to inflict the penalties of treason could not be assumed by the Council without statutory sanction. The Act was in fact restrictive in the same way as 3 Henry VII C. 1 was, and in part, at any rate, for the same reason. As in the case of the more famous measure, the exceptional power granted was never used.

The third specialized sub-committee was what came to be known as the Court, or Council, of Requests, established mainly for the hearing of poor men's civil suits, with which the Chancery was becoming overburdened. This Committee of Council appears to have been created by Richard III, but lapsed on the accession of Henry VII owing to the hostility of Parliament. After a few years he revived it. The Council had always been concerned with the settlement of poor men's causes, as the King was bound by his coronation oath to do justice to all his people when they could not get it from subordinate authority or were too poor to sue at Common Law, but there does not seem to have been any regular organization for dealing with them until Yorkist times. It seems that poor men's petitions were either passed on to the appropriate Court with instructions that they were to be settled expeditiously, in spite of any technical errors in presentation, or, very occasionally, heard by those members of the Council who happened to be present with the King. In 1390 an ordinance had been drawn up which provided that all bills of the people 'of less charge' might be heard by the Keeper of the Privy Seal and such Councillors as were available. Professor Baldwin has pointed out that the words 'of less charge' might refer to the nature of the petitions, and not to the poverty of the people who brought them, but it seems improbable, and the fact remains that the Keeper of the Privy Seal continued to be associated with poor men's causes. Indeed, he came to be considered to be the poor men's Chancellor, and the Court of Requests the poor men's Chancery.[1]

In the first year of Richard III, a second Clerk of the Council was appointed, one John Harington, expressly "for his good service before the lords and others of the Council, especially in the custody, registration, and expedition of bills, requests and supplications of poor persons."[2] This looks as though closer and more frequent attention to this class of business must be ascribed to the preceding reign. The establishment of an organization of some kind for the regular trial of these cases seems however to have been due to Richard. According to a journal kept by the two burgesses for Colchester of the proceedings in the Parliament of 1485, a bill was passed on December 10 of that year abolishing the 'Court of Requests'. The creation of the Court was apparently attributed to

[1] J. F. Baldwin, op. cit., p. 259.
[2] Ibid., p. 435.

Richard III.[1] The bill did not become law. Presumably Henry refused his assent. But he was not sufficiently firmly on his throne to be able to ignore the hostility of Parliament, and allowed the Court to lapse till 1493, when, having made peace with France and defeated his enemies at home, he silently revived it. The Court had no fixed habitation, but moved about with the King. In the circumstances it was difficult to organize a regular membership, as the personnel accompanying the King on his peregrinations varied greatly. However, an effort was made in 1494 to secure a measure of continuity. The Bishops of Bath, Exeter and Rochester were to attend after Easter; the Prior of S. John's and Lord Broke from a fortnight after Easter until August; Lord Daubeney during August, September and October; Robert Rude from February to July; and certain other four knights, the Master of the Rolls (who was the Chancellor's second-in-command for civil judicial purposes) and three doctors of law—i.e. Civilians—for the whole year. It is not likely that all these persons were in practice present at the times laid down, and others certainly sat on occasion, including the notorious Empson, but it seems that some degree of continuity and specialization was ultimately achieved, as among the 172 Councillors whose names are known, twelve are said to have sat in the Court of Requests, whose presence was not recorded at any ordinary meeting of the Council.[2] It is therefore possible that the separation of the personnel of the 'Court' of Requests from that of the King's Council proper had begun.

The procedure was probably always the same—that for summary causes in the Civil Law. The petition was always addressed to the King, never to the Council or the Chancellor. The defendant put in an answer. Sometimes the proceedings were extended by a 'replication' by the petitioner, and a 'rejoinder' to the 'replication' by the defendant. Witnesses could be produced and the parties themselves were examined. Summons was usually by writ of privy seal. In the early days of the Court, certainly till the end of Wolsey's time, hearings were expeditious and cheap, and though delay and its natural concomitant, expense, later showed themselves, the proceedings of the Court always remained cheaper and more easily intelligible than those at Common Law.

[1] Growth of the Court of Requests, A. F. Pollard, *E.H.R.*, 1941.
[2] A. Conway, *Henry VII's Relations with Scotland and Ireland*, Cambridge, Appendix XLI, p. 229.

Its benefits were nominally restricted to poor persons and servants of the King, but tended in time to be extended to cater also for "abbots, knights, esquires and other wealthy complainants"[1] which undoubtedly exacerbated the hostility of the Common Lawyers to the institution.

The progress made in the reign had been considerable. The criminal jurisdiction of the Council had been continued—partly, though to no great extent, by the undifferentiated King's Council itself, which did most of its judicial work at headquarters, in the Star Chamber; and partly by the Council learned in the law. The tone of Parliament as regards outrage and intimidation had changed since Lancastrian days. The influence of the great baronial houses, exhausted by the civil wars and by the confiscations which followed Bosworth, was no longer preponderating. The economic condition of the country had begun to improve, and most people were thoroughly tired of disorder, which, however, had by no means disappeared. Parliament seems therefore to have been anxious to strengthen the arm of the executive authority, and even to have thought that Henry was not going fast enough in the suppression of turbulence. In 1496 an Act initiated by the Commons was passed to deal more effectively with riots and unlawful assemblies. By the terms of this measure, in particularly heinous cases, or in those in which the rioters were over forty strong, the judges were directed to certify the fact, and remit the chief offenders to the King's Council for punishment. In 1504 Parliament complained that "little or nothing is or hath be doon" about liveries and maintenance, and that year saw the passing of the Act, *De retentionibus illicitis*. It is to be noted that both rioting and the giving of liveries were among the offences made punishable by 3 Henry VII C. 1, which is another indication of the practical ineffectiveness of that measure. It seems possible that in 1504 Henry decided that more active measures were necessary, and decided then to appoint the sub committee of Council 'learned in the law', the records of which begin in that year.

In addition the Council of the North continued to function, at least in Yorkshire, both as a supplement to the ordinary criminal jurisdiction, and as a local Court of Requests, until the end of the reign. It was, however, prematurely abolished in 1509, for reasons which are not obvious. The Council of Wales and the Marches was

---

[1] William Lambarde. Quoted *Tudor Constitutional Documents,* ed. J. R. Tanner, p. 307.

F

also established on a permanent basis, and dealt with both crime and the civil suits of the poor.

On the civil side, the Chancery functioned as a true Court of Equity, both for the trial of cases for which no provision or inadequate provision had been made in the Common Law, and for the reversal of clearly inequitable decisions; and civil justice was made more readily accessible to the poorer classes all over the country by the restoration and reorganization of the 'Requests' jurisdiction.

Henry VII had certainly advanced from the beginning made by the Yorkists, but perhaps the epithet 'strenuissimus' applied to him by John Skelton,[1] better describes his efforts to rehabilitate the finances of the Crown, than the achievement of the other half of his task, the restoration of order.

[1] John Skelton, *Latin epitaph of Henry VII*, Complete Works, ed. P. Henderson p. 434.

CHAPTER IX

THE RESTORATION OF ORDER
(III) WOLSEY

FROM 1516, when he received the Great Seal, the government of the country was in the hands of Cardinal Wolsey, who ruled in Henry's name, and with his entire approval, until his fall in 1529. He had more power than anyone in England had ever had. For practical purposes he was both King and Pope. He had, moreover, a tremendous personality, which made up for the enduring lack of physical force at the disposal of the monarchy, and enabled him to use his spiritual and temporal supremacy to advantage.

The best account of the startling change in the atmosphere of the Council Chamber brought about by the great Cardinal is to be found in the satires of Skelton, Henry VIII's court poet. Wolsey dominated his colleagues absolutely. He was a bully, rough, rude, overbearing, and no respecter of persons. In the Star Chamber, where most of the work of government was done, he would brook no factious argument or contradiction, thumping the table with his rod, plucking great nobles by the hood, or even by the ear, and beating down all opposition with blistering torrents of abuse.

"He triumpheth, he trumpeth, he turned all up and down with skirgalliard![1] proud palliard![2] vaunt perler![3] ye prate!" There is no wonder that he was extremely unpopular with his colleagues, cringe to him though they did in the days of his glory. Skelton loathed Wolsey, but his description of his manners and language is probably a true one. It must be remembered that he wrote his mordant satires, 'Colin Clout', 'Speak, Parrot', and 'Why Come ye not to Court' for the delectation of people who knew Wolsey well personally, as he did himself, and though the views he expresses on his policy and achievements may well be dismissed as due to personal bias, it is not conceivable that he would have made absurd mis-

[1] Rascal.
[2] Rogue.
[3] One who speaks out of turn—'avant parler'.

statements about the outward and visible signs of the Cardinal's character.

With such as Wolsey in the Chair, with the even more formidable King behind him, there was little chance of the Lords of the Council supporting their erring brethren or interceding for highly placed ruffians. Not even the great nobles of the turbulent north could disregard with impunity what he called 'the New Law of the Star Chamber'. New it certainly was in scope and vigour.[1]

Skelton, who was a conservative in all things save rhyme and metre, obviously had some sympathy with the bold bad baron, and seems to have regretted the reduction of the aristocracy to a dull level of quiet respectability.[2] Hall, on the other hand, though he also disliked Wolsey, felt bound to pay a reluctant tribute to his effectiveness as a restorer of order. He praised his stern repression of the prevailing crime of perjury, and also the swift and condign punishment which he meted out to the organizers of riot and intimidation.[3]

The Council was kept busy in term-time trying cases in the Star Chamber. Most of its leading members remained all the year round at Wolsey's call, and did not attend the King in his Court or on his peregrinations, which aroused the intense indignation of Skelton. As late as 1526 Cap. 74 of the Council Ordinances laid down that twenty persons, beginning with the Cardinal himself, should attend on the King. This was mere camouflage. In practice members mostly of only minor importance, especially household officials, such as the Comptroller, the Vice-Chamberlain, the Dean of the King's Chapel, and the Captain of the Guard were available for duty with His Majesty.[4]

The duties of such Councillors as remained with the King included "the hearing of poor men's complaints on matters of justice", in

---

[1] *Letters and Papers, Henry VIII*, Vol. II, Appendix 38, p. 1559. "Albeit there hath lately, as I am informed, been a fray betwixt Pygot your sergeant, and Sir Andrew Windsor's servants, in the which fray one man was slain. I trust at the next term to learn them the new law of the Star Chamber, that they should beware how from henceforth they shall redress the matter with their hands." Wolsey to Henry VIII.

[2] "The Earl of Northumberland   Dare not look out at door
 Dare take nothing on hand!   For dread of the mastiff cur
 Our barons be so bold   For dread that the butcher's dog
 Into a mousehole they wold   Would worry them like an hog."
 Run away and creep
 Like a meiny of sheep!

[3] Hall, *Henry VIII*, ed. T. C. and E. C. Jack, 1904, Vol. I, p. 152.
[4] J. R. Tanner, *Tudor Constitutional Documents*, pp. 220–1.

which subject Wolsey was always particularly interested. It seems that 'Requests' Jurisdiction had been, to some extent at least, delegated to a perhaps rather fluid sub-committee of Council as early as the reign of Henry VII; but Wolsey appears for a time to have restored it to the whole Council, apart from the few cases heard from time to time by the members of Council with the King. From the wording of the order of 1516 or 1517 appointing the White Hall in the Palace of Westminster as the place for hearing poor men's causes it appears that Wolsey had been hearing them in the Star Chamber (where all the work of the Council at headquarters was still done, and not merely the trial of criminal cases). This is corroborated by Hall, who says that the poor brought suits in vast numbers, and that the Cardinal grew weary of hearing them, and so delegated this duty to 'divers under courts'. The chief of these was to sit in the White Hall, in the Palace of Westminster, and was definitely a specially selected Committee of Council, eight in number, of whom four were ecclesiastics. Others, according to Hall, were held in the Lord Treasurer's Chamber; at the Rolls; and in the room of the King's Almoner.[1] These three were, it seems, soon abandoned, and the headquarters tribunal for the hearing of poor men's causes was permanently located in the White Hall, and became definitely split off from the undifferentiated Council sitting in the Star Chamber.

It is certain that Wolsey did very greatly increase this side of conciliar judicial activity, as he did the exercise of its criminal jurisdiction. The sessions in the White Hall of Westminster seem to have continued regularly—at least in term-time—after 1516, and in addition provision was made for the continued reception of poor men's bills of complaint by the Council with the King'ubicunque fuerit'. He also instructed the Justices in other parts of the country, at any rate in the distant north, where the Council was not re-established till 1525, to receive and hear them. The Earl of Surrey wrote Wolsey on August 14, 1523 that he had spent four days with the Justices at York "hearing infinite complaints of the poor people, which could not have been fully redressed in a month."[2] This may well have been one of the factors, if not the main factor, which decided Wolsey to reconstitute the Council of the North. The Council of Wales and the Marches also gave relief in civil matters to the poor on the spot. Lord Ferrers, in a letter to Thomas Arundel

[1] Hall, op. cit., Vol. I, p. 152.
[2] *Letters and Papers, Foreign and Domestic*, Vol. III, Part 2, § 3240, p. 1346.

in 1526 wrote that it had been announced that no one living in Wales and the Marches should be summoned to appear at Westminster, but that all causes should be determined by the President and Council. Proclamations to that effect were accordingly made in Westminster Hall and in Wales, "which have caused daily prayers to be made for Wolsey in these parts."[1] The area concerned included the border counties of Shropshire, Worcestershire, Herefordshire and Gloucestershire.

The revived Council of the North was staffed mainly by Wolsey's servants. Its authority was restricted to Yorkshire save in matters of justice, in which its members co-operated with the Wardens of the Marches of the North (Cumberland, Westmorland, and Northumberland). Of its seventeen members five were Canon Lawyers and five Common Lawyers, two of whom were Chancery practitioners, and hence trained in equity. It seems clear that Wolsey's Council of the North was intended primarily to administer cheap and equitable civil justice, and to be what it was often called at the time a 'Court of Requests'.

The making of justice accessible to the poorer classes seems, indeed, to have been one of Wolsey's main domestic preoccupations. The Venetian, Sebastian Giustinian, reported to his Government in 1519 that "he favours the people exceedingly, and especially the poor, hearing their suits and seeking to despatch them instantly. He also makes the lawyers plead gratis for all paupers." The great increase in 'Requests' jurisdiction may have been one of the reasons which made him odious to the upper classes generally, and not merely to those members of them who appeared before him on criminal charges.

As Chancellor, Wolsey was the head of the legal hierarchy, and in the time allowed to him he made it known that he was. He could not give much time to the hearing of cases in Chancery, though Cavendish, his servant and biographer, says that he usually spent the early part of the morning in the Court.[2] None the less, there seems to be little doubt that he increased, sometimes arbitrarily, the scope of equity. The organization and expansion of the 'Requests' jurisdiction, however, gave the Chancery some relief, and Wolsey also

---

[1] *Letters and Papers, Foreign and Domestic,* Vol. IV, Part I, § 2201, p. 980.

[2] "and that done he would repair into the Chancery, sitting there till eleven of the clock, hearing suitors and determining of divers matters." He had done much before, so could not have sat there for more than one or two hours. George Cavendish, *Cardinal Wolsey,* ed. S. W. Singer, Chiswick 1825, Vol. I, p. 44.

regularly employed the Master of the Rolls as his deputy for the hearing and decision of causes. It is clear that the comparatively amicable relations which had usually subsisted between the Chancellor and the Common Law judges, who in the past had frequently been consulted on points of law, ceased during Wolsey's tenure of the office. There seems to be no reason to believe that he was influenced by the mediaeval conception, still dominant in St. Germain's dialogue between Doctor and Student, that the function of equity was to bring, when required, positive laws into agreement with the Law of God, and of Nature and Reason. He appears rather to have regarded the 'artificial reason' of the Common Law with impatient contempt, and to have held that it should be overridden whenever possible.[1] There seems to be no doubt that he bullied the judges and lawyers as he bullied the Lords of the Council.[2]

To sum up, in the thirteen years of his ascendancy, Wolsey scotched the long rooted evil of anarchic violence, though it still flourished in Wales and the Marches, and was capable of showing signs of life on occasions elsewhere for generations after.

Fuller provision had been made for the poorer classes who had

---

[1] "It was indeed significant to see this fellow, ignorant of law sitting in Court and pronouncing judgment; although at first he was assisted by the lawyers, who by ancient custom were his assessors, he began to hear and dispose of many cases which which were neither finished nor properly conducted. He forbade other cases, in which there was no doubt about the law, being taken in judgment, cut short disputes, punished with vigour the parties to the suit as bringing forward before the judges trumped up charges; at the same time he severely rebuked the negligence of the judges who heard the cases and who had not assessed damages fairly. And so the government of Wolsey had for the common people a shadowy appearance of justice, which indeed because it was only a shadow, quickly disappeared." Polydore Vergil, *Anglia Historia*, Camden Series, Vol. LXXIV, p. 231.

See also George Cavendish, *Cardinal Wolsey*, ed. S. W. Singer, Chiswick 1825, pp. 216–7, "Law without conscience is not good to be given unto a king in counsel to use for a lawful right, but always to have a respect to conscience before the rigour of the Common Law."

[2] "Judges of the Kinge's Lawes
He counts them fools and daws
Sergeants of the Coife eke
He saith they are to seek
In pleading of their case.
At the Common Place
Or at the Kinge's Bench
He wringeth them such a wrench
That all our learned men
Dare not set their pen

To plead a true trial
Within Westminster Hall.
In the Chancery where he sits
But such as he admits
None so hardy to speke
He saith "Thou hoddipeke.
Thy learning is too lewd
To seek before Our Grace"
And openly in that place
He rages and he raves
And calls them "cankered Knaves."

J. Skelton, 'Why Come ye not to Court', *Collected Works*, p. 328.

some property or interest to protect, but insufficient means to seek legal remedy in the Courts of Common Law.

Abuse of legal process he checked only temporarily by the fear which he inspired. It could be decisively defeated only by reform of the process itself. In the sphere left to it the Common Law was as formal, dilatory, and expensive as ever. It is possible that Wolsey's stupendous energy and force of character might have enabled him to make radical alterations in the whole administration of justice, had he not been so deeply immersed in foreign affairs. There seems to be no doubt that he was keenly interested. One Robert Ryche addressed him in 1528 on the subject, "knowing Wolsey's great zeal for the reform of the Common Law, which, however, he is too busy to attend to, begs to be called before him that he may declare the abuses that are daily used and suggest remedies."[1] Whether Wolsey heard him or not we do not know, but by that time his day was nearly done.

[1] *Letters and Papers, Henry VIII*, Vol. IV, No 4937.

CHAPTER X

HENRY VIII AND THE CESSATION OF PROJECTS OF LAW REFORM

THE danger to the Common Law disappeared with Wolsey. He was succeeded as Chancellor by Sir Thomas More, a Common Lawyer, and the son of a Judge of the Common Bench, and as Henry's right hand man by Thomas Cromwell, his secretary. Henry had decided to use Parliament, and especially the House of Commons, as his instrument for the conduct of his quarrel with the Pope. Cromwell was the first man to become Chief Minister because he was the best choice for the task of managing the House of Commons. The Common Lawyers were strongly represented in that House, and were far too influential a body for Henry to risk alienating. Nor is there any reason to believe that the reform of the Common Law in the interest of the general public lay near his heart. It seems indeed that none of the Kings of this period, or their ministers (with the exception of Wolsey) were hostile to the Common Law as such. They had recognized that the failure of the courts, both civil and criminal, to do justice and enforce the law, had to be rectified, but no far-reaching or radical scheme of reform seems ever to have been considered. It might perhaps even be said that the remedies adopted were for the most part intended to bring about a state of affairs in which the ancient English legal system could once more work smoothly and effectively, though in a somewhat restricted sphere. What did interest Henry was the maintenance and if possible the extension of the power of the Crown, and, like his predecessor, he seems to have regarded the Common Law as adapted, or at least adaptable, to that end.

Henry's extravagance, and his embroilment in useless and noxious wars with France, soon dissipated the fortune his frugal father had left him. Before the final breach with Rome placed the vast wealth of the monasteries within his grasp, he turned like his father before him to the improvement of his feudal revenues as the most likely method of increasing his regular income. This he decided to do by

73

stopping the loophole provided by the practice of creating uses. He eventually achieved his end, in a watered down and inefficient form, after a long period of diplomatic manoeuvring, by the passing of the Statute of Uses in 1536.

The history and development of the Use is a long and complicated one, and here a brief explanation of the point at issue must suffice.[1] The use was a form of trust. Three parties were involved—the owner of the land, his feoffee or feoffees—usually there were more than one—to whom he had made it over, by conveyance or 'bargain and sale' for the use of the third party, who would actually receive the profits of the estate. The third party—the 'cestui que use' might be himself, his children or other relatives, a friend or friends, an institution or a corporation. One purpose of the Use was to enable holders of freehold property to dispose of it as they pleased in spite of their legal inability to devise their lands by will. No testamentary restriction applied to the 'cestui que use', who could dispose of his interest in the estate (not the estate itself) by will as he chose. But in a large number of cases the main advantage of the creation of a use lay in the fact that the King, or other lord, could be defrauded of his feudal dues. All the incidents of tenure, wardship, marriage, primer seisin, livery, escheat and forfeitures, to which the heir to the estate would have been liable, had he retained the legal ownership, could be evaded by the appointment of a number of feoffees, with provision for their replacement when necessary. They therefore became to all intents and purposes an immortal corporation, and as they were the legal owners, the feudal incidents in practice lapsed. It was presumably this possibility of avoiding the obligations of military tenure which determined the attitude of the Common Law, which regarded the feoffee, who had seisin of the property, as the owner of the estate. The 'cestui que use' was recognized only incidentally. There was nothing illegal about the creation of a use, but it was not enforceable at Common Law, and the feoffee, if he were unscrupulous, could treat the estate as his absolute property, and ignore the terms on which it had been made over to him. The Chancellor therefore stepped in, as the upholder of the claims of conscience and fair dealing, and the enforcement of uses and trusts early became an important part of his equitable jurisdiction.

[1] For fuller account see Holdsworth, Vol. V, pp. 407–80; T. F. T. Plucknett, *Concise History of the Common Law*, pp. 544–69, and The Revival of Feudalism in Early Tudor England, J. B. Hurstfield, *History*, Vol. XXVII, 1952.

Henry had originally intended to abolish uses altogether, but the opposition was too strong, and the attempts of 1529 and 1532 both failed. The landowners were hostile, because they would no longer be able freely to bequeath their lands, and also because what they stood to lose by enfeoffments to uses by their tenants, they could much more than make up by defrauding the King, who always lost, as he was always lord and never tenant. The lawyers shared their resentment, as though the Common Law recognized only legal estates, the arrangement of complicated enfeoffments gave them much lucrative business. Here, then, again the nobility and gentry and the lawyers were allies, and the task of getting a measure of which they disapproved through Parliament, even in an emasculated form, taxed the ingenuity of Henry and Cromwell to the utmost.

Henry was well aware of the unpopularity of the administration of civil justice, and of lawyers, among all those who had sufficient property to be interested, but insufficient means to run 'the course of the Courts', though too much to qualify for the Court of Requests. As prosperity increased, and what may be called a lower middle class had begun to multiply rapidly, the unpopularity grew. The spreading influence of the Renaissance was also inclining a section at least of the better educated towards the desirability of a 'Reception' of Roman Law in England. Thomas Starkey, who became Henry VIII's chaplain, and who worked from 1534 or 1535 in close collaboration with Cromwell, wrote his 'Dialogue between Cardinal Pole and Thomas Lupset', in which, *inter alia:* he summed up the views of the English humanists on the Common Law, some time early in 1535. "Who is so blind", he wrote, "that seeth not the great shame to our nation, the great infamy that remaineth in us, to be governed by the laws given to us of such a barbarous nation as the Normans be? Who is so far from reason that considereth not the tyrannical and barbarous institutions, infinite ways left here among us, which all should be wiped away by the receiving of this which we call the very civil law?" Lupset thinks that this would be difficult to bring to pass, but Pole replies, "Nay, nay, Master Lupset, easier than you think of. The goodness of a prince would bring this to pass quickly; for the law of itself is easier to learn than is ours in the French tongue. Wherefore there lacketh nothing but authority to put it into effect; the which I pray God we may once see."[1] The

---

[1] *Dialogue between Cardinal Pole and Thomas Lupset.* Thomas Starkey, Early English Text Society, 1878, Extra Series No. XXXII, p. 92.

dialogue was not published at the time, nor indeed for many years after, but the existence of views like those ascribed to Pole and Lupset was doubtless widely realized, and was known to Henry.

In 1534 Henry had received a petition complaining against abuses in the courts, and the impossibility of remedy owing to there being so many lawyers in the House of Commons. The petition ended by asking for legislation to fix lawyers' fees. The attention which Henry paid to this seems to have alarmed the lawyers in Parliament, and at the same time he scared the gentry by instituting rigorous inquiries into the settlements of their estates. He was also able to play upon the jealousy of Chancery which was increasingly felt by the Common Lawyers as the business in that Court increased. Also the equitable treatment of uses had recently come in for a particularly violent attack in the pamphlet entitled "A Replication of a Sergeante at the Lawes of England", in which uses were described as deliberately designed to rob the King and his subjects of the dues guaranteed to them by the Common Law, and as being contrary to reason and also to the Law of God.

By 1536 the Lawyers had been brought to a more tractable frame of mind by fear of projects of far-reaching reform. Even so the bill dealing with uses had to be drafted in such a way as to placate them. Uses were not abolished, but converted into legal estates, the holders of which were responsible for all the liabilities of the original owner. The Common Lawyers scored by the fact that uses had now become fully recognizable at Common Law, at the expense of Chancery, which did not, however, lose all this valuable part of its jurisdiction, as uses for a term of years were not affected by the Statute, and these soon became common. The drafting moreover allowed for the development of a large variety of evasive interpretations, of which the lawyers were not slow to take advantage. Maitland describes the Act as "that marvellous monument of legislative futility, the Statute of Uses, the Statute through which not mere coaches and fours, but whole judicial processions with javelin men and trumpeters have passed and repassed in triumph."[1] For some time however, the King gained, as well as the Common Lawyers, but the landowners lost, as they were no longer able to bequeath their lands by will. It seems likely that they had been persuaded by the lawyers to withdraw their opposition to the measure. Resentment however soon

---

[1] F. W. Maitland, *Collected Papers*, Cambridge 1911, Vol. II, Law of Real Property, p. 191.

became widespread when they recognized the extent of their dis-
ability, and the repeal of the Act was one of the demands made by
the rebels of the Pilgrimage of Grace. In 1540, after Henry had been
confirmed by Parliament in his possession of the wealth of the
monasteries, he felt it to be both possible and prudent to do something to placate the gentry, and by the Statute of Wills allowed them
a considerable measure of freedom in devising their freehold estates.

Henry had wished to follow the Statute of Uses, and make it as
lawyer-proof as possible, by a comprehensive Statute of Enrolments,
whereby efficient arrangments were to be made for the registration
of all conveyances. The lawyers were hostile to such a simpli-
fication, there being no set off as in the Statute of Uses, nor did the
gentry approve the publicity which would have been given to their
secret and involved land settlements, and it was rejected by Parliament, which adopted instead a restricted makeshift which could
easily be evaded. Had it passed, Burton's lament that "he that buys
and sells a house must have a house full of writings" would not have
been penned.[1]

The history of the Statute of Enrolments, and the protracted
negotiations necessary to secure the passing of the Statute of Uses,
show clearly that the growth of the power of Parliament, and
particularly of that of the Lower House, which was due to Henry's
use of it, meant also the consolidation of the already formidable
position held by the Common Lawyers. Henry had already found
it necessary to compensate them for Wolsey's high-handed treatment
by the revolutionary step of appointing Common Lawyers to the
office of Chancellor. Professor Plucknett considers that the Statute
of Uses was passed on the understanding that thenceforward no
attempts were to be made to reform the Common Law.[2] Certainly
no measure designed to that end was put forward throughout the
remainder of the period. So far from the Common Law being
endangered, as Maitland thought, in the middle fifteen-thirties, it
was confirmed and strengthened in its ancient courses. Doubtless
there was a considerable diminution in the business coming before
the Common Law Courts, owing to the popularity of the conciliar
tribunals and the expanding jurisdiction of the Chancery, but legal
practitioners, at least of the superior grades, were most amply

---

[1] Robert Burton, *Anatomy of Melancholy*, Democritus to the Reader, pp. 92 et seq.
(Shilleto's edition).
[2] T. F. T. Plucknett, op. cit., p. 554.

compensated by a proclamation issued by Henry VIII in 1546, which laid down that no one who was not a Common Lawyer trained in an Inn of Court was eligible to plead in the Common Law Courts, the Chancery, the Star Chamber, or the Courts of Duchy Chamber, Augmentations, Surveyors, Tenths and First Fruits, and Wards and Liveries unless appointed by the Chancellor (now and almost always a Common Lawyer) and the two Chief Justices, with the advice of the Benchers of the Inns of Court. This meant a rapid decline in the prospects of Civilians. Some years later Dr. Thomas Wilson complained that it was hardly worth while to study the Civil Law, so few were the cases for which their services were required.[1] Henry's foundation of Professorships of Civil Law at Oxford and Cambridge was due to his need for the services which trained civilians could give in negotiations with foreign powers, whose law was the Law of Rome, not to a desire to provide practitioners for the Conciliar Courts. The study of the Canon Law was forbidden. The cessation of the Year Books in 1535 "at the moment when the Henrican terror was at its height" was, so Maitland thought, "dramatically appropriate".[2] But the Year Books were being replaced by reports of judicial decisions, instead of records of pleadings. Written pleadings drawn up outside the Court had replaced the old system of oral pleadings in the presence of the judge, and the decision of a case had become the object of interest to the law student rather than the minutiae of procedural altercations. The replacement of the old-fashioned Year Books by more scientifically arranged volumes of law reports, one of the more famous of which, that of Dyer, started with cases of 1537, cannot be said to indicate a danger point in the history of the Common Law. On the contrary it may be said that the danger disappeared in 1529. The failure of Katherine of Aragon to produce an heir was responsible not only for the breach with the Papacy, but also, owing to the consequent aggrandisement of the House of Commons, for making a Henrican reformation of the law a political impossibility.

[1] Thomas Wilson, *A Discourse of Usury, 1572.*
[2] F. W. Maitland, *English Law and the Renaissance,* p. 77.

CHAPTER XI

THE ORGANIZATION OF THE COMMON LAW COURTS AND CHANCERY DURING THE LATER TUDOR AND STUART PERIODS

BEFORE proceeding to consider the developments, both judicial and political, arising from Henry VIII's appeasement of the Common Lawyers, it is desirable briefly to examine the organization of the Courts. It was highly defective, and there is no doubt that it greatly increased the delay and expense of civil litigation at Common Law and in Chancery. It was therefore responsible for much discontent, and in consequence added to the embarrassment of the executive government. The scandals of the Chancery, which began to emerge in the latter part of Henry's reign, were also partly due to the same cause.

The poverty of the Crown was ultimately responsible. The judges were paid an inadequate salary, which was, moreover, frequently in arrears, and most of the ministerial hierarchy, on whose efficiency and honesty much depended, were not paid at all. On the contrary they had to purchase their places.

The remuneration of the judges might not seem at first sight to be absurdly low. The Puisne Judges of both the King's Bench and Common Pleas received £128 6s. 8d. a year, the Chief Justice of the Common Pleas £141 13s. 4d., and the Chief Justice of the King's Bench £208 6s. 8d. The Barons of the Exchequer, however, received only £40, and the Chief Baron £100.[1] These sums would have to be multiplied many times to represent their purchasing power today, but it is to be remembered that the judges were appointed only from the small society of sergeants-at-law. In Fortescue's time there was "no advocate in the whole world who enriches himself by reason of his office as much as the sergeant."[2] A century later, Chancery practice was probably much more valuable,

---

[1] *Desiderata Curiosa*, Queen Elizabeth's Annual Expenditure, Liber II, p. 67.
[2] Sir John Fortescue, *De Laudibus Legum Angliae*, ed. S. B. Chrimes, Cap. XLIV, p. 125.

but the sergeants never starved. There is no doubt that the earnings of the leaders of the Bar, many of whom became sergeants and ultimately judges, were always high, and by the end of the sixteenth century enormous. Some were said to make from £20,000 to £30,000 a year.[1] The foundation of the fortunes of many noble families was laid by an ancestor's successful career in the law, particularly in the sixteenth century. Coke, says Wilson "within these ten years in my knowledge was not able to dispend above a hundred pounds a year, and now by his owne lands, his coyns, and his office, he may dispend between twelve and fourteen thousand." He certainly acquired more than fifty manors. Ellesmere left his son a huge fortune. Not all of their wealth came from their practice in the courts. They had excellent opportunities, owing to their business connections with the aristocracy and gentry, for making profitable speculations in land, the market in which had developed rapidly after the dissolution of the monasteries.

The judges, therefore, were not expected to be content with their official salaries and allowances. Their income was largely supplemented by fees received from litigants, not in any way for personal consideration, but as automatic payments for the sealing of judicial writs. This practice was responsible for the efforts made to attract business, for the hostility of the judges to the Chancery, the prerogative civil courts, especially the Court of Requests, for the rivalry in the later seventeenth century between the King's Bench and Common Pleas, and for the constant failure to weed out or reject false and frivolous cases.

The sale of offices was another source of income, especially to the Chief Justice of the Common Pleas and the Chancellor, who had gained control of the bulk of ministerial appointments in their courts. Some of them were extremely valuable, and Holdsworth considers that this patronage by the end of the seventeenth century had become more lucrative than salary and fees put together.[2] These offices were regarded as freeholds, and subject to the conception of tenure. They were the properties of the persons holding them. This notion, drawn like so much else from the mediaeval land law, lasted till well into the nineteenth century, in spite of its patently deplorable consequences. In the middle of the eighteenth century

[1] R. H. Tawney, The Rise of the Gentry, *Economic History Review*, 1941, and T. Wilson, *The State of England 1600*, Camden Miscellany, Vol. XVI, 1936.

[2] Holdsworth, *History of English Law*, 4th edition. Vol. I, p. 255.

Blackstone wrote that "Offices, which are a right to exercise a public or private employment, and the fees and emoluments thereunto belonging, are incorporeal hereditaments." One result was that it was most difficult, indeed practically impossible, to to divert fees from an office which had originally been entitled to them, even though that office was no longer capable of doing the work paid for, and in fact did not do it, and even though the work no longer required to be done, and in fact was not done. The litigant still had to pay. All Chief Justices and Chancellors seem to have had the same ideas on the subject as Lord Keeper North, or at least to have found it desirable to acquiesce in the continued existence of these abuses. He had, said Roger North, no inclination to retrench superfluous offices or to deprive their holders of their accustomed perquisites, to which, in his opinion they were justly entitled, by custom and connivance, if not strictly by law.[1] More personal reasons may have swayed the Lord Keeper, perhaps subconsciously. The Six Clerks of the Chancery had long been holders of highly lucrative sinecures. What had been their work had long been done by deputies appointed by themselves and by attorneys. They were "always disposed to keep the judge in good humour and prevent alterations to their prejudice" and on one occasion they presented the Lord Keeper with a present of £1,000 "which he took as an instance of their respect, without regard to or knowledge of any other design or intention of theirs."[2] Not only in the Chancery, but in all courts it was customary for the judges to accept valuable presents from the clerical establishment "On New Year's Day, or otherwise".[3]

Moreover, apart from the receipt of large thankofferings from time to time, as most of the more valuable clerkships were in the gift of the Chancellor and the Chief Justices, or rather were sold by them for very high prices, it naturally followed not only that they had no inclination to move for the abolition of those which had become redundant, but also that they were not likely to take steps to curtail

[1] *Lives of the Norths,* ed. Jessop, Bohn 1890, Vol. I, p. 264.

[2] *Lives of the Norths,* Vol. I, p. 371.

[3] See the *Autobiography and Correspondence of Sir Simonds D'Ewes, Bart.,* ed. J. O. Halliwell, London 1845, Vol. I, p. 177.

D'Ewes' father was one of the Six Clerks. From 1622–1630 he gained £15,166. He had paid nearly £5,000 for his sinecure, and "many new year's gifts and other charges were also incident to his office, besides some large bribes towards his latter time extorted from him and his fellows". Charles had extracted £10,000 from them in 1627.

G

the fees which the holders collected from the public, as that would make the office less valuable to the holder, and hence less profitable to the vendor. It seems possible that the long life of the conception that these clerkships were freehold property, and that their holders were as much entitled to the fees and emoluments traditionally attaching to them as a landlord to his rents, was due at least in part to the fact that the profits of their disposal were considered as being a part of the legitimate income of the chief judicial officers of the country. Chief Justice Hale, in the second half of the seventeenth century, expressed as an obstacle to his proposal for reconciling the quarrels between the King's Bench and the Common Pleas over jurisdiction in the classes of civil cases which they shared in common, the fact that the existing constitution of the King's Bench was not adapted to the changes which he had in mind, as they would mean the abolition of some offices, the loss of fees by others, and the disappearance of a considerable source of income to the Chief Justice and Judges.[1] Holdsworth says of the Chancery "An attack on one of these officials (the twelve Masters of Chancery and the Six Clerks) always appeared to those interested in the patronage, not as the act of a man dismissing a useless servant, but as the act of depriving a man of his freehold. It was on this ground that the Six Clerks escaped abolition in the time of the Commonwealth."[2]

There was indeed a temptation to increase the number of clerk-ships when possible.[3] The only effective limitation was the fact that an existing official could and did object to the appointment of additional staff to assist him on the ground that his fees would be reduced. Normally, therefore, the difficulties caused by the increase of business, and the lengthy elaboration of procedure were met by the original clerk himself appointing a deputy or deputies, whom he underpaid or did not pay at all, and left to do as well as they could for themselves. In due course the work of some of these offices came to be performed entirely by deputy, and then the resulting sinecure became a prize to be competed for by needy courtiers or influential

---

[1] Lord Chief Justice Hale, A Discourse concerning the Courts of King's Bench and Common Pleas, *F. Hargrave's Tracts Relative to the Laws of England 1787*, p. 372.

[2] Holdsworth, *History of English Law*, Vol. I, p. 424.

[3] "The Judges to increase the Fees of the Court and make Offices Great, which were in their disposal to sell to those which would give most for them (as Horses in Smith-field) have appointed 20 or 40 Offices and Places in a Court where the business might be done by 3 or 4 Honest Clerks—for where the Judges take fees, the Love of Interest overcomes all other loves."   John Cook to the Lord Deputy of Ireland, August 6, 1655.

officials, which, in the conditions of the time, made the possibility
of reform still more remote. Much public discontent was aroused,
and in 1551 an Act was passed forbidding the sale of judicial offices,
but all those at the disposal of the Courts of King's Bench and
Common Pleas were excluded from its purview and there is no
doubt that it was generally altogether ineffective. Vested interests
were too deeply entrenched.

The Clerks of all the Courts—Common Law and Chancery—were
also closely, even organically, connected with the lawyers—especially
the attorneys—practising in them. Clerks acted as attorneys, particularly in the early part of the period, and attorneys as clerks. The
Protonotaries, or Chief Clerks in both the King's Bench and
Common Pleas, did not merely enter pleadings in the rolls of the
Court, but were consulted on technical points, even by the judges.
The preparation of judicial writs, which had been one of their
functions, was entirely taken over by the litigants' attorneys, though
the protonotary still received fees for doing it. The filazers, who also
dealt with writs and common form pleadings, originally did much
work later done by attorneys.[1] In the Court of Chancery the Six
Clerks, who were supposed to write and check writs before they were
sealed, acted as solicitors[2] to litigants until the pressure of business

---

[1] "Attorneys are such as have by experience learned and do know the orders and
manner of proceeding in every Courte, wheare they serve. These purchase out the
writtes and process belonging to their Clyent's case, there they see their suits that they
be not hindered by negligence, they pay the fees belonging to the Courte, and
prepare the Cause for judgment." R. Robinson, Camden Miscellany, 1953, Vol. XX,
p. 2.

[2] Solicitors first appeared in the Court of Chancery and in the Star Chamber.
Their dealings were more with advocates, than with clerks. Their functions in 1592
are described in "A briefe Collection of the Queen's Majestie's most High and most
Honourable Courts of Recordes" by R. Robinson (Camden Miscellany, 1953,
Vol. XX). "The Solicitors are, or should be, Learned in the Lawes of the Realme,
who being rightly instructed of the suitor's case do more skilfully enforme the
Serjeants and Counsellors-at-Lawe in the same." At the time they seem not to have
enjoyed a good reputation. Lord Keeper Egerton expressed the view that they were
not warrantable by any law, that they were 'caterpillars del commonweale' and that
maintenance would lie against them. (Les Reportes del cases in Camera Stellata
1593–1609: John Hawarde, ed. W. P. Baildon.) Hudson was of the same opinion,
"In our age," he wrote, "there are stepped up a new sort of people called solicitors,
unknown to the records of the law, who, like the grasshoppers of Egypt, devour the
whole land: and these were express maintainers and could not justify their maintenance upon any action brought. . . . These are the maintainers of causes and devourers
of men's estates by contention, and prolonging suits to make them without end."
W. Hudson, A Treatise on the Star Chamber, Collectanea Juridica, London 1792,
Vol. II, pp. 94–5.

made this no longer possible. There is no doubt that throughout the period (and for long after it) the clerks and underclerks of all kinds worked hand in glove with the less reputable members of the legal profession, the efforts of both alike being directed to the protraction of proceedings and the multiplication of fees. The clerks benefited largely by the number and length of the declarations and pleas which they copied and entered, and the art of spinning them out developed to such an extent in all courts (even in the Star Chamber) as to become a well-nigh intolerable burden on the litigating public.[1] Its continuance is an illustration of the difficulty of achieving even an obvious and minor reform. This could not be done without the co-operation of advocates and attorneys, but the judges cannot escape responsibility. Unforunately those far higher in the scale than underclerks or pettifogging attorneys were interested in the protraction of proceedings, especially in Chancery. They succeeded in their endeavours.

The numbers of attorneys, many of whom were poorly qualified "and had but the skill to know to what office to send for a process"[2] had increased enormously, particularly in the sixteenth and seventeenth centuries, and it was impossible for a large proportion of them to earn a living honestly. The Presiding Officers of the Courts exercised no supervision over their doings, with rare exceptions, and as a result the unholy alliance between the attorneys and the clerical establishment had an astonishingly free hand. Their misdeeds did not stop at the multiplication of processes. The author of the tract on the jurisdiction of the Court of Chancery, written possibly, by a Master in Chancery, some time in the early seventeenth century, went so

[1] Carey complained in 1627 of the "making of long bills in the English Courts, full of matter impertinent. . . and the underclerks with their large margins, with their great distance between the lines, with protraction of words, and with many dashes and slashes put in place of words, lay their greediness open to the whole world; and I have heard many say that they are as men void of all conscience, not caring how they get money, so they have it. . . . I did see an answer to a bill of forty of their sheets, which, copied out, was brought to six sheets; in which copy there was very sufficient margin left, and good distance between the lines (they were paid by the sheet, not the word). Hereby every man may see how infinitely, by the abuse of petty clerks (the Court of Chancery swelling and ready to burst with causes, the Star Chamber, and the rest), the whole kingdom is robbed as it were; for that copy which should have cost but four shillings cost four nobles. But as for the higher clerks and officers, they would fain have this foul and unconscionable fault amended, because it maketh nothing for their profit." Carey, The Present State of England, *Harleian Miscellany*, Vol. III, p. 210.

[2] Considerations touching the Amendment of Lawes, Chief Justice Hale. Printed in *A Collection of Tracts Relative to the Law of England*, F. Hargrave 1787, p. 28b.

far as to say that in the Courts of Common Law not one judgment in a hundred was pronounced in Court, or considered by the judges, but was entered in the rolls by attorneys without the judge's knowledge, especially in cases where the plaintiff's attorney had collusively retained, or acted in collusion with, the attorney for the defendant, who agreed, presumably for a consideration, to the claim made against the person whom he was supposed to represent.[1] Once this agreement had appeared in the record—which was normally irrefutable—it was extraordinarily difficult to upset. The author of the tract was undoubtedly a Civilian, and as such unfriendly to the Common Law, and he must have exaggerated greatly, but it is none the less true that rascalities of this kind could be and were perpetrated. The protonotaries should have been able to check this practice, but they too relied largely on attorneys to increase their gains. Chief Justice Hale says that the multitude of attorneys who infested the courts of King's Bench and Common Pleas arose principally from the demand caused by "the scambling and scuffling between the protonotaries, every one striving to get as many as he can to bring grist to his mill."[2] Attorneys were officers of the Court in which they worked, and were appointed by the judges. Complaints against their excessive number had been made as early as the beginning of the fifteenth century, and in the seventeenth were loud and general, but nothing was done, and the judges were to blame.[3]

The power of the vested interest, so strongly represented in Parliament, which enabled these abuses to flourish, is strikingly indicated by Bishop Goodman, in his History of his own Times.

[1] A Vindication of the Judgment given by King James in the Case of the Jurisdiction of the Court of Chancery, *Collectanea Juridica*, Vol. I, pp. 74–5.

[2] Chief Justice Hale, Considerations touching the Amendment of Lawes, p. 285.

[3] Burton described the legal underworld of his day as "a general mischief in these our times, an insensible plague, and never so many of them, which are now multiplied as so many locusts, not the parents, but the plagues of the country, and for the most part a supercilious, bad, covetous, litigious generation of men, a purse milking nation, a clamorous company, gowned vultures, qui ex infuria vivant sanguine civium, thieves and seminaries of discord; worse than any pollers by the highway side . . . that take upon them to make peace, but are indeed the very disturbers of one peace, a company of irreligious harpies, scraping, griping catchpoles. (I mean our common hungry pettifoggers; I love and honour in the mean time all good laws and worthy lawyers that are so many oracles and pilots of a well governed commonwealth) without art, without judgment, that do more harm, as Livy said, quam bella externa, fames, morbive, than sickness, wars, hunger, diseases; and cause a most incredible destruction of a commonwealth." Robert Burton, *Anatomy of Melancholy*, Shilleto's edition, pp. 92 et seq.

He said of lawyers "if once they could but stint the royal prerogative, which they would pretend to be an exorbitant power, and much
against the liberty and freedom of the subject, then the supreme
judicatory was in them, and they, under the colour of interpreting
the law and keeping the forms of their Court, giving ear to their
favourites, and discountenancing such as did not depend upon them,
they became more absolute Governors than any legal prince in
Christendom. So that to be a lawyer, which I did conceive to be
ministerial, was indeed to be a governor of one's country."[1] John
Clapham, who had belonged to Burghley's entourage, wrote that in
his time there was no profession held in higher reputation than the
Common Lawyers, many of whom had made fortunes. Some, he
admitted, deserved praise, but a large number had devoted themselves to practices and devices which resulted in legal remedy
becoming worse than the disease. It was in fact much better for a
man to submit to the loss of a part of his estate than to risk losing it
all by claiming his rights in court. He also complained of the evils
caused by the sale of judicial and ministerial offices.[2]

The judges were practically never influenced by base motives in
giving their decrees, and the leaders of the bar enjoyed as a rule a
reputation for probity, but it can be said that from the Chancellor
and the Chief Justices down to the humblest filacer's underclerk,
none were altogether free from what would now be called a
measure of corrupt interest. In the case of the upper grades of the
hierarchy, particularly the judges, the ancient doctrine of office as
freehold, and the sanctity of long continued tradition served as
convenient justifications for permitting innumerable petty rascalities,
and many serious ones, to continue and to be sheltered under their
aegis. They were too secure in their positions and too influential for
the King and his Council, even under the great Tudors, to venture

---

[1] Cf. Lord Brooke, *A Treatise of Monarchy*, ed. Grosart, Vol. I, § VII. He writes, on
lawyers—

> As making judges and not princes great
> Because that doubtful sense which they expound
> Raiseth them up above the Prince's Seat
> By offering strength, form, matter, and a ground
> To fashion all degrees unto their end,
> Through men's desires which covet law to friend."

and T. Wilson in *The State of England 1600* (Camden Miscellany, XVI, 1936).
"These lawyers are growne so great, so rich, and so proud that no other sort dare
medle with them."

[2] John Clapham, *Elizabeth of England*, ed. Evelyn Reed and Angus Reed, University of Pennsylvania Press, 1951, p. 66.

directly to intervene and compel them to put their house in order. There can be no doubt that the scandalous maladministration of the courts added considerably to the widespread and growing grievance caused by the involved intricacies of the English legal system.

CHAPTER XII

THE COURT OF REQUESTS FROM THE REIGN OF HENRY VIII

THE Courts mainly affected by the triumph of the Common Lawyers in Henry VIII's time were the Court of Requests, the Chancery, and the conciliar jurisdiction of the King's Council in the Star Chamber. The least influenced by Common Law theory and practice was the Court of Requests, where Common Lawyers never enjoyed a monopoly, either on the Bench or at the Bar. Until the end of Henry VIII's reign it was staffed by a standing Committee of Council. The Court was extremely popular, and the pressure of business seems to have been too much for the Lords of the Council who found themselves being converted into whole time civil judges. Shortly after Henry's death two trained lawyers were appointed to assist them, and they gradually displaced the laymen entirely. They were known as Masters of Requests. In Elizabeth's reign it was found necessary to appoint two more—Masters of Requests Extraordinary—who became permanent in the reign of James I. As a rule two were Civilians and two Common Lawyers[1]—though sometimes laymen were appointed. Burghley sat as a Master of Requests in 1549, and Sir Lionel Cranfield, later Earl of Middlesex, in 1613.[2]

Throughout the period, particularly in the reigns of Elizabeth, James I and Charles I, the business of the Court was varied and voluminous. Up till the end of the sixteenth century its operations did not arouse the hostility of the Common Lawyers, as it was regarded (and rightly) as an integral part of the King's Council, and also the class of business dealt with was not normally lucrative. The gentry had always objected to it. Part of Wolsey's unpopularity was almost certainly due to his interest in 'poor men's causes'. Protector Somerset, who sympathized with the underdog, had used it to

---

[1] James I never appointed Civilians as Masters of Requests, presumably in order to placate the Common Lawyers. Charles I, however, is said by Clarendon to have promised Archbishop Laud to appoint none but Civil Lawyers.

[2] I. S. Leadam, *Court of Requests*, Selden Society, 1898. A list of Members of the Court is published in the Introduction, pp. CX–CXXIV.

assist copyhold tenants and others to combat the exactions of the landlords. Somerset's action gave rise to great indignation, as the landlords had been hard hit by the great price rise, and was one of the causes of his fall. However the Court of Requests continued to function unchecked and unhampered, and the enmity of the Common Lawyers was not fully manifested for another generation. Probably the main reason for its appearance was the growing interest in constitutional law, and the opportunities given by the development of a Committee of Council into a fully professionalized law court for doubts to be thrown upon its legal position. This aspect is more fully considered below.[1] A subsidiary reason may have been the fact that comparatively well-to-do persons had succeeded in getting their cases heard by it, though its jurisdiction was supposed to be strictly limited to those too poor to sue at Common Law, and to servants of the King ordinarily attendant upon his person or in his household. This seems to have begun, probably in a minor degree, late in the reign of Henry VIII, and the practice was responsible not only for rousing the antagonism of powerful enemies in Westminster Hall, but also for some deterioration in the conduct of the Court. It was 'a court of conscience appointed to mitigate the rigour of proceeding in law' and its procedure was "altogether according to the process of summary causes in the Civil Law".[2] But when well-to-do people began to make their appearance as plaintiffs, the necessity of keeping costs low—which was best effected by expedition ceased to be regarded as essentially necessary. Though the costs of litigation in the Court of Requests always compared favourably with those in the Common Law Courts, they undoubtedly became considerable, at least until the reign of Charles I. Originally pleadings had often—perhaps usually—been limited to the plaintiff's petition, and the defendant's answer. Later replications by the plaintiff, rejoinders by the defendant, and lengthy interrogatories, upon which the parties and their witnesses were examined, were added, and the case might be sent to a magistrate of the locality concerned, either to settle it, or report. In 'Observations of the proceedings in the Court of Requests addressed to the Earl of of Northampton' some time after 1608[3] it was stated that delaying

---

[1] See Chap. XV, pp. 215-7.

[2] I. S. Leadam, *Select Cases in the Court of Requests*. Selden Society, 1898, Introduction, XXI.

[3] I. S. Leadam, op. cit., Introduction, p. XCVI.

tactics were being adopted by defendant's Counsel, with the object of vexing and wearying plaintiffs, usually poor men, particularly by raising points of law in demurrers. All this is reminiscent of Common Law (and later Chancery) practice. The Court of Requests sat only in the law terms,[1] so trivial interruptions in the course of a hearing could spin it out for a long time. As early as 1543, the King and Council had issued a directive to the Court, in which clauses appear which were obviously intended to keep down the costs and protect illiterate litigants. Lawyers who failed to do their duty by their clients were to refund the fees they had taken, and "charges without need" were to be avoided. Another cause of delay, due also to the protraction of proceedings, is to be found in the fact that though the Judges of the Court were permanent, lack of continuity was a subject of complaint. The same case was frequently heard by a succession of judges, which caused confusion and contradictory orders.

From 1590 onwards the Common Law judges did their best to make the work of the Court impossible by a constant stream of prohibitions, and for most of James's reign it was struggling for existence. In Charles I's time, however, the judges had been tamed, and when the Earl of Manchester became Lord Privy Seal in 1627 a new era of vigour and efficiency began. He revived the ancient practice of presiding over the Court himself with highly beneficial results, and it continued to do good work for the remainder of its existence.

[1] J. R. Tanner says (*Tudor Constitutional Documents, p.* 300) that "the Court of Requests did not, like the Star Chamber, keep fixed terms, but was accessible to suitors throughout the year; and provision was made for securing the attendance of a sufficient number of Councillors at all times to hear cases." This is true only of the early days, and before the dominance of the professional element. The law terms were observed from 1522 onwards.

CHAPTER XIII

THE COURT OF CHANCERY IN THE XVIth AND XVIIth CENTURIES

WELL before the end of the sixteenth century the Chancery was handling a greater volume of causes, and causes of far greater value, than all the Courts of Common Law at Westminster.[1] This was one of the reasons for its undoing, or rather of the undoing of its suitors. The personnel of the Court was not increased to keep pace with the ever-growing tide of litigation, and prolonged delay, in itself inequitable, inevitably became a scandal. The state of affairs described by Roger North after the Restoration dated back to the time of Elizabeth. "The truth is," he wrote "a Court such as that is, with officers and fees proper for a little business such as the judiciary part anciently was, coming to possess almost all the justice of the nation, must needs appear troubled. For it began with common petitions, and the defendants' answer wrote on the back of it."[2]

The Chancellor was the sole judge. He alone came to be called 'the Keeper of the King's Conscience'. He was the busiest man in the kingdom. Apart from his judicial work in the Chancery, which remained open throughout the year, and his general control of the great office both on its Common Law and Equity sides, he was a prominent member of the King's Council. In term-time he presided over the Court of Star Chamber. His attendance in Parliament, where he presided over the House of Lords, was invariably necessary, and after 1529 Parliaments met often. After Wolsey's time he had ceased to be the King's Chief Minister for all the business of the nation, foreign and domestic, but even Wolsey had found it impossible efficiently to combine the duties of Chancellor with the conduct of foreign affairs, and left large arrears. These were cleared off by Sir Thomas More, who was able to devote more time to the judicial side of his duties, but under his successors the pending list

[1] 32,240 suits were instituted in the reign of James I—or about 1,464 a year (C. P. Cooper, Public Records 1,356 n.).
[2] *Lives of the Norths,* ed. Jessop, Vol. I, p. 257.

grew to be unmanageable. Wolsey started the practice of delegating judicial duties to the Master of the Rolls, who was the chief of the Masters in Chancery, and in the seventeenth century he became the unofficial deputy of the Chancellor, but his position was not regularized until 1729.[1] The relief this afforded to the Chancellor was wholly inadequate.

Another fertile cause of delay was due to the development of Chancery procedure by the Common Lawyer Chancellors. Judgments were still based on general principles of abstract justice, as understood by the individual Chancellors till the end of the period and for long afterwards, in spite of the natural craving of the Common Lawyers, whose influence was predominant in Chancery from the middle of the sixteenth century, for 'certainty'. In 1615 Lord Ellesmere stated the obvious truth "for that men's actions are so diverse and infinite that it is impossible to make any general law which may aptly meet with every particular act, and not fail in some circumstances."[2] After all, it was to correct the failures of 'general Law' that the equitable jurisdiction of the Chancellor had arisen, although towards the end of the seventeenth century, the principles governing the administration of equitable justice was beginning to show signs of fixity, and precedents had for some time been quoted.[3] Blackstone could say as late as the middle of the eighteenth century that the administration of equity depended 'essentially upon the circumstances of each individual case, and there could be no established rules and fixed precepts laid down without destroying its very essence.'[4] Not until the time of Lord Eldon (Chancellor from 1801–27 after having been Chief Justice of the Common Pleas) did the workings of conscience give place entirely to deduction from rigid doctrines and precedents. Then, had the King and his Council retained their ancient powers and obligations, petitions would

---

[1] Philip Yorke, Earl of Hardwicke, *A Discourse of the judicial authority belonging to the office of the Master of the Rolls*, London 1727, esp. pp. 8 and 9.

[2] Lord Eldon, in the Earl of Oxford's case, quoted Holdsworth, Vol. I, p. 453.

[3] Norburie wrote in James I's reign "Some judges, when they seem doubtful what to determine in a cause, will be inquisitive after precedents; which I cannot conceive to what purpose it should be unless that being desirous to pleasure a friend, and the matter being of the nature that they are ashamed to do it, they would fain know whether any before them have done so ill as they intend to do." (The abuses and remedies of Chancery, *Hargrave's Law Tracts*, p. 446.) This seems hardly fair. The cause was undoubtedly the Common Law Chancellor's natural craving for written authority.

[4] Blackstone, *Commentaries I*, pp. 61–2.

undoubtedly have been made to them for equitable relief against decrees in equity. But they had not, so the strange process, due to the long lived influence of mediaeval education, whereby the Common Law, which had originated from appeals to the equitable justice of the King, became so fixed and rigid as to make equitable relief to those suffering from its decisions a necessity, was not again repeated.

But the Common Lawyers, in spite of the fact that there was no certainly deducible issue to any case, nor precedents to aid them in their search for certainty, did not cease to endeavour to find it. Their guide was the Dialogue between a Doctor of Divinity and a Student of the Laws of England, by Christopher St. Germain, a Common Lawyer, the first editions of which were published in 1523 and 1530. St. Germain, who was well read in the Canon Law, believed that equity was complementary to positive law, like most English lawyers before and after him, however narrow their views may have been as to the limits of its application.[1] His guiding principle was that of the Canon lawyers, the operation of conscience. There was nothing novel about that—all the Chancellors since the time of Richard II had relied upon it. What was new was the laying down of conditions justifying the application of the general principle to the decision of particular cases.

St. Germain had been a student of the later scholastic philosophers, notably the great jurist John Gerson.[2] Gerson had naturally drawn largely from Aristotle, whose works were far better known in his time than they had been in the thirteenth century. Aristotle insists upon the necessity of observing in the greatest detail all the circumstances of every individual case. When this has been done, the syllogistic, or dialectical, method might be employed to extract conclusions. What St. Germain did was to substitute the Canon Law principles of Reason and Conscience for Aristotelian dialectic. This appealed strongly to the Common Law Chancellors and Advocates, who were always most chary of taking responsibility. They were therefore naturally sympathetic towards the idea of collecting data on which to base a decision, in default of the pos-

[1] But see the 'Replication of a Sergeante at the Lawes', written about the same time as S. Germain's dialogue "The lawe of the Realme is a sufficient rule to order you and your conscience what ye shall do in everie thing and what ye shall not do." *Hargrave's Law Tracts*, pp. 322–55.

[2] See Vinogradoff, Reason and Conscience in 16th century jurisprudence, *L.Q.R.*, XXIV, 1908.

sibility of deduction from written authority. The aim therefore of the Chancellors after the middle of the sixteenth century was to strive after the Aristotelian ideal of complete knowledge of all the facts. Then, and then only, a thoroughly informed conscience could be relied upon to give a fair judgment. In brief, the attainable end of substantial justice was replaced by devotion to the ideal of absolute justice. A further advantage in the eyes of the Common Lawyers was that the ancient elasticity of the principles of Reason and Conscience, depending, according to Selden, "on the length of the Chancellor's foot" was very largely destroyed.

It may be said that the root cause of the failure of the Common Law was the application of Aristotelian dialectic to what was regarded as established authority as the method of arriving at decisions without observation of the circumstances of the case under consideration. Direct observation was considered to be a delusion and a snare. This would surely have horrified the 'Philosopher of Fact'. On the other hand, the catastrophic disaster which befell English Equity was due, in the prevailing conditions of the Court of Chancery, to the belated recognition of the Aristotelian insistence on the need for complete factual investigation. Aristotle however would surely have held that neither part of his method was applicable to the endless individual diversities of litigation.

The development of a systematic and highly elaborate equity procedure in the place of the old rough-and-ready methods proceeded rapidly in the later sixteenth century and was completed in the seventeenth. Many points in it were reminiscent of the Common Law, even in the pleadings, though the Common Law system aimed at the production of a single issue, while that of the Chancery was designed to lay every aspect of the case before the Court.[1] That was a natural consequence of the dominating position of Common Lawyers in the Court after the reign of Henry VIII. Apart from Mary's reaction in favour of ecclesiastics every Chancellor after 1529 had been educated in an Inn of Court, with the exception of Hatton in Elizabeth's reign, and Bishop Williams in that of James I. Some had been Chief Justices. Since 1546 Common Lawyers had enjoyed a monopoly of practice at the Chancery Bar. The resultant admixture of Common Law theory and practice, including even the develop-

---

[1] For a detailed account of Chancery procedure, see Holdsworth, *History of English Law*, Vol. IX, pp. 342–78; and Bentham, *Introductory view of the Rationale of Evidence*, Works, ed. Bowring, VI, 43.

ment of case law, into a system supposedly designed to secure the perfection of equitable justice led to almost inconceivable delay, expense, and inefficiency. A contested suit in equity frequently lasted from twenty to thirty years, and the costs might consume the entire value of even a large estate. The lawyers rejoiced in a system which remunerated them so handsomely, and the Masters of Chancery ("a sort of under judge" as Bentham called them) and their clerks made it their business to protract proceedings and multiply forms and processes as much as possible. All the officials of the Courts from the Masters downwards were appointed for life and held their offices as freeholds. They were remunerated entirely by fees. "Hence", as Holdsworth says, "although there was stagnation enough, and abuses enough in Common Law procedure, there was never acquiescence in any such systematic injustice as was perpetrated by the procedure of the Court of Chancery, in its endeavour to accomplish by means of an utterly inadequate staff, and an obsolete machinery, an unattainable ideal of complete justice."[1] The staff was not merely inadequate. It was grossly corrupt, and the Chancellors had not the time—nor with few exceptions, apparently the desire—to supervise their activities, or even to check the delaying tactics almost habitually employed by Counsel.

George Norburie wrote some time in the reign of James I "How cometh it to pass that this honourable Court should be traduced as it is, and have so many foul aspersions thrown on it, as to be termed a dilatory Court where a suit will last longer than a suit of perpetuanza or a suit of buff? I answer in one word 'Councellers'."[2] Motions were constantly made for the investigation of a point by one of the Masters in Chancery,[3] or by a Commission appointed to take evidence in the country, employing the unique Chancery methods, justly described by Holdsworth as futile and absurd. Interlocutory orders multiplied. Even after a decree had been pronounced, the Chancellor could often be persuaded to reopen the whole case on some fresh surmise being put forward. The examination of accounts could be queried and spun out till it lasted for years, until, as Norburie said, the unfortunate suitor "hath scarce a round shilling left in his purse." "A cause in Chancery", said William

[1] Holdsworth, *History of English Law*, Vol. IX, p. 373.
[2] George Norburie, Abuses and Remedies of Chancery, *Hargraves Tracts*, p. 436.
[3] Most of the Masters in Chancery were Civilians throughout the period. Laud is said by Clarendon to have persuaded Charles I always to appoint Civilians to half the Masterships in Chancery.

Cooke in 1642 "though never so plain, after a reference or two, and a generation or pedigree of orders, the controversy will become so intricate that, the merits of the case being lost, all the labour lies in the management of reports and orders."[1] The Registrar's Office was able to hold up cases almost indefinitely unless suitably sweetened, and a brisk trade called 'heraldry' sprang up—the purchase for substantial sums of precedence on the cause list. Multiplicity of hearings and orders were greatly to the advantage of the clerks, as they meant multiplicity of fees. Mention has already been made of their relations with solicitors and attorneys, and nothing effective was ever done to check this evil, though some Chancellors, especially Bacon, were, like Lord Keeper North fifty years later "sensible of the prodigious injustice and inequitable torment inflicted upon suitors by vexatious and false adversaries, and other chicaneurs that belong to the Court."[2] False and frivolous cases were legion. Norburie goes so far as to say that out of ten bills brought into the Court, hardly three had any colour or shadow of just complaint, but were brought merely to harass an enemy.

Apart from being used as a stick wherewith to chastise an opponent, Chancery was the frequent recourse of unscrupulous people, who had properly failed at Common Law.[3] As John Cooke wrote in 1655 "A man takes away my coat, which I recover at Law, the defendant upon some pretence of a bargaine will sue me in the Court of Equity, and when I have spent £20 I can never get my coat again, but it may be I may recover £10 damages and costs. Had I not better observed the Lord Christ's command literally, Matthew V. 39, 40, 'if any man will sue thee at the law, and take away thy coat, let him have the cloak also'."[4] Nothing was done to check this evil. On the contrary, injunctions to stay proceedings at Common Law were frequently issued on wholly inadequate grounds, on the request of dishonest litigants. False and frivolous cases produced fees as well as fair ones, and the defects which caused such bitter complaints in the sixteenth and seventeenth centuries, endured, apart from the brief Interregnum, till the nineteenth.[5]

---

[1] Vindication of the Professors and Profession of the Law. William Cooke 1642. Cited, Holdsworth, Vol. I, p. 427.

[2] *Lives of the Norths*, Vol. I, p. 296.

[3] *Hargrave's Law Tracts*, p. 434.

[4] John Cook to the Lord Deputy of Ireland, 1655.

[5] The remarks of William Haslewood, a barrister, written in 1829 might well have been penned two centuries before—"Complaints are loud and general, not only of the

"The agent of the new monarchy in respect of the conflict of laws was the Chancellor." Henry VIII's policy of appeasement of the Common Lawyers, (dictated entirely by political considerations) did to some extent resolve this conflict, but at the price of creating and fortifying a scandal which has never been surpassed or even approached in the history of legal institutions.

---

harassing delay and ruinous expense which constantly prevail, but of the defective trials and conjectural judgments, the groundless yet protracted litigations and the unmerited imprisonments which too often occur in Courts of Equity. Chance, more blind than justice, must have no inconsiderable share in dispensing orders and decrees, which are seldom founded on guidance, properly so called. Dishonest debtors and reckless adventurers seem invited to the profitable exercise of falsehood and fraud: while persons of an opposite character shrink from a conflict which may consume a fair estate, and by long suspense and ultimate disappointment, may subdue a spirit of more than common firmness." *Heads of a Bill for an Effectual Reform of the Court of Chancery;* offered for consideration by William Haslewood of the Inner Temple, London 1829, p. 1.

There is no need to quote here Dickens's well-known tirade in Bleak House, but the following is also true of 17th-century conditions—"Many a suitor has impatiently traversed this little street again and again in breathless agitation: the dun, the bailiff, and the hired perjurer may be daily found there, and perhaps more misery, injustice, and rapacity have originated in its neighbourhood than in any other part of London. But if Chancery Lane affords instances of the foulest practices, of gross immorality, and roguish cunning, its outward appearance does not belie the character which it is said to bear; it is almost invariably dirty under foot in Chancery Lane." 1843. London, ed. C. Knight, Vol. IV, p. 370.

CHAPTER XIV

THE CRIMINAL JURISDICTION OF THE KING'S COUNCIL FROM 1540

HENRY VIII, like all his predecessors, had always had what was in effect a 'privy' council, though in Wolsey's time it was practically limited to Wolsey himself. Sir Robert Wingfield wrote in 1534 that he had been a member of the King's Council for twenty years and of the 'private council' for fourteen. In March 1538 one Thomas Darly was described officially as the Clerk of the Privy Council, but the full reorganization of conciliar arrangements was not achieved until 1540, when nineteen members were appointed to it. Professor Pollard thinks that the appointment of 'ordinary councillors' ceased some time in Edward VI's reign.[1] Surviving 'ordinary councillors' may sometimes have been called in under Henry VIII and Edward VI for special purposes or employed in subordinate conciliar bodies such as the Council of the North, but it seems certain that after 1540 the King's Council was simply and solely the Privy Council.

So much confusion has been caused by failure to understand the real purpose and meaning of the reorganization, designed, as Sir Philip Hoby recommended in 1538, "to withdraw the King's Council more secret together," and to keep it in closer touch with the King, that it is perhaps advisable to attempt a recapitulatory survey. Since Edward III's day, the Council's normal habitat was the Star Chamber in the King's Palace of Westminster. When the King was abroad or on tour some of his Councillors accompanied him. The remainder stayed behind at Westminster and carried on the day-to-day administration. Business of any kind mostly administrative, but sometimes judicial, was carried on, by the same people in the same room or rooms known as the Star Chamber. Apart from Henry VII's experiments with subcommittees for particular purposes, this simple arrangement for the transaction of ordinary governmental business continued until after the fall of Wolsey.[2] In his time the majority

[1] The Council, A. F. Pollard, *E.H.R.*, 1922.
[2] Except for the trial of poor men's Causes.

of the regular Councillors, including almost all the great officers of state, remained at headquarters, sitting in the Star Chamber at Westminster, where they carried on the administration of the country under the direction of Wolsey, and disposed of a greatly increased quantity of criminal judicial work. A few councillors, mostly household officials of minor public importance, accompanied the King, largely *honoris causa*, on his peregrinations.

After Wolsey's disgrace, Henry, with the aid of Cromwell, the Secretary, began to take much more personal interest in governing. In 1540 a completely new system was finally inaugurated. Instead of a large amorphous body of Councillors, some of whom were used a great deal, others only on occasion, with a small unofficial inner ring who enjoyed the King's confidence, a compact all purposes Council, of nineteen members,[1] all of whom enjoyed at least some of his confidence, was appointed. It ceased to sit in the Star Chamber at Westminster, except when the King was there, but carried on its multifarious duties at whatever palace the King happened to be using at the time, Windsor, Greenwich, Whitehall, Hampton Court, so as to be within call whenever he had any communications to make to it, or when ever it desired to obtain his instructions. Henry never troubled himself to go to ordinary meetings—nor did Mary or Elizabeth. They made their wishes known through the Principal Secretary, who from Cromwell's time till the days of the Stuarts became unofficially the monarch's chief minister.

In term-time a number of these privy councillors were deputed to sit in the outer Star Chamber at Westminster, for the trial of criminal cases in public. They were reinforced for this purpose by the Chief Justices or other judges. This was the King's Council in the Star Chamber, and, apart from the judges, it and the Privy Council consisted of the same people. There was no difficulty in seconding a few privy councillors for Star Chamber duties. Normally from four to six were sufficient. The sessions were held only in term-time, i.e. for about twelve weeks in the year in all, and though Wolsey had begun by devoting four days a week during that period to Council trials, later two days, Wednesdays and Fridays, were found sufficient. Also, as all preliminary work, interrogatories and so on, was done outside the court by the Clerk and his deputies, and cases were not laid before the Lords of the Council and judges

---

[1] The number fell as low as 11 in Queen Elizabeth's reign, but rose to over 30 in the time of Mary and again under James I and Charles I.

till ripe for decision, the sessions lasted only from nine till eleven in the morning.

So far as the existing attendance records show, no one, certainly from the time of Elizabeth, apart from the judges, seems ever to have sat to do justice in the Star Chamber who was not a member of the Privy Council. Professor Pollard has suggested that the dislike and distrust with which the King's Council in the Star Chamber was regarded in the reign of Charles I was due to the fact that he used the same persons for executive work in the Privy Council and for judicial duties in the Star Chamber.[1] But Charles was guilty of no innovation here. The solitary case of Davison, Elizabeth's unfortunate Secretary, when only three of the thirteen judges were Privy Councillors, which has caused some misunderstandings, is to be explained by the supposition that it was not an ordinary Star Chamber trial at all, but a trial by special commission, for which the members of the tribunal were appointed *ad hoc*.

The simple fact is that the King as in the time of Fleta, still 'had his Court in his Council'. There was never any idea of the separation of executive and judicial functions. The Privy Council, sitting as such, and without the assistance of the judges, or of counsel, did a great deal of judicial work in an arbitrary and summary way, and constantly sentenced offenders to whipping, or to the pillory, with or without the loss of one or both ears, or ordered the wearing of papers inscribed with the nature of the offence, or committed them for unspecified and often protracted periods to the Tower, the Fleet, the Marshalsea, the Counter, Newgate, Bridewell, the Gate House, or the Porter's Lodge, and even on occasion to the coal hole at Windsor.[2] It sometimes fined people, though not often. All classes of persons were liable to punishment at the Council Table—peers of the realm, bishops, gentry, merchants and tradesmen, and also humble folk of all sorts. 'Lewd words' reflecting on the character or policy of the monarch were very severely punished, and so were insults to peers, members of Council and officials. Offenders against the statutes concerning religion, both Roman Catholic recusants and Puritan nonconformists, frequently felt the weight of the Privy Council's displeasure. So did dishonest officials. Perjurers,

[1] The Council, A. F. Pollard, *E.H.R.*, 1922.
[2] Thomas Yemens of Beksley, beside Oxford, "roving about the country and at last sent uppe to the Council, seemed to be a foolish prophet and talked of the Scripture, so . . . having been moved from the Porter's ward to the Coal House at Windsor, came to himself". *Acts of the Privy Council 1542–7*, p. 249.

however, were almost always publicly sentenced in the Star Chamber and also juries who gave false verdicts. In 1581 a Grand Jury in Staffordshire was summoned before the Council for failing to find true bills against notorious recusants. The Council ordered them to appear before the Judges of Assize and acknowledge their contempt and offence "which if any of them refuse to do, bonds to be taken from them for their personal appearance before their Lordships in the Starre Chamber the first day of the next terme . . . where their lordships intend to proceed against them for their offence according to justice."[1]

Riots were quite often dealt with by the Privy Council, both those due to aristocratic turbulence, and those caused by the indignation of the victims of enclosures. The enclosers too were apt to be summoned before the Council, as were engrossers and other types of anti-social offenders. Offences against Royal Proclamations were more often punished at the Council Table than in the Star Chamber. Common Law and statutory offences were often sentenced summarily, including ordinary crime, attempted murder (or suspicion of murder), burglary, coining (which frequently attracted the Privy Council's attention), and, often, piracy. Occasionally judicial authorities were ordered to execute the summary sentences of the Council, or were given clear instructions as to what was expected of them. In 1593 some butchers were hauled up for having killed and offered flesh during Lent "contrary to her Majesty's commandment and a Proclamation inhibityting the same". Orders were sent to the Justices of the Peace of Middlesex "to cause them to be indicted by a jurie, and to fyne them in good round sommes of money for these their contempts, which shall be converted to the use of maymed soldiers, in respect of their disobedience, and suche as shall refuse to paie soche sommes set upon them you shall by vertue hereof comytt them to pryson untill they have satysfied the same."[2] Sometimes unusual punishments were inflicted. "Two very lewd and loose fellows" (George Ellis and Walter Pepper) who had already been censured in the Star Chamber for forging the signatures of some of the Councillors on warrants, being again found guilty of the same offence, were sent by the Privy Council from the Marshalsea, where they were confined, and where apparently they were able to continue their nefarious activities, to Sir John Hawkins to work in

[1] Acts of the Privy Council, 1581.
[2] Acts of the Privy Council, 1592–3, p. 166.

chains as galley slaves, and, for a time at least, on a low diet.[1]
Torture was sometimes applied to suspects in order to make them
confess. In 1586 the Council ordered the Lieutenant of the Tower
to re-examine one Matthew Beaumont concerning the robbery of
Lady Cheek, "and of suche other matters whereof the truth is to be
drawn from him, and finding him obstinate, to trie him in some
reasonable manner by torture on the rack what he can further dis-
close of anie robberies by him and others in anie sort committed."[2]
Torture was apparently never used by the Council in the Star
Chamber.[3]

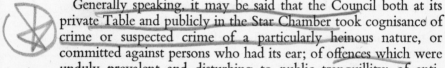

Generally speaking, it may be said that the Council both at its
private Table and publicly in the Star Chamber took cognisance of
crime or suspected crime of a particularly heinous nature, or
committed against persons who had its ear; of offences which were
unduly prevalent and disturbing to public tranquillity; of anti-
social conduct; of sedition, or insubordination to constituted
authority; slander; political or religious dissidence, and disobedience
to Proclamations. A great many cases of all kinds were initiated in
the Star Chamber by bills or petitions of private persons, but apart
from these, whether a case was heard at the Council Table, or in the
Star Chamber depended entirely on the need for publicity. The
Council decided when once a case had come to its notice, by
information or report, whether to hear it in private, or to reserve it
for public trial in the Star Chamber. There are a number of examples
recorded in the Acts of the Privy Council. In 1578 "a supplication
having been exhibited containing very foul matter against one Miles
Lakin, the said Lakin's Lewdness is found to be such as deserveth
open punishment."[4] The case was accordingly remitted for hearing
in the Star Chamber. This is an example of the quality of the offence,
and not of the offender being considered as qualifying for public
trial. On the other hand, one Thomas Coe, in Newgate for debt,
who had made false accusations against a great number of honest
and worthy citizens, had railed against a Councillor of the Board
(i.e. one of the Privy Council) and had striven to break the locks and
doors of his prison, was dealt with summarily, because "the fellow
is so base and contemptible, he is not worthy of a proceeding in the

---

[1] *Acts of the Privy Council*, 1592–3, p. 487.
[2] *Acts of the Privy Council*, 1586–7, p. 56.
[3] *Pace* A. V. Dicey (*Privy Council*), who quotes the case of Guy Fawkes. But he
was tried by a Special Commission, not by the Council in the Star Chamber.
[4] *Acts of the Privy Council*, 1577–8, p. 237.

Star Chamber, and yet it is very meete that he should be punished, and therefore we have thought it good to require you (the Recorder of London) to take notice of it, as of a direction from this Table, and to give present order that he be sharply whipped in such manner as may best serve for example, and for his amendment, if it may be."[1] In 1618 the Council decided that imprisonment in Newgate—perhaps the most dreaded of all the prisons—was not a sufficient punishment for one Captain Le Grys, who had given false information against Lady Markham—saying that she had expressed a wish that the Gunpowder Plot had been successful—so transferred him to the Fleet to await trial '*ore tenus*' (i.e. he had confessed his fault) in the Star Chamber.[2] The Council sometimes transferred cases—at any stage in the proceedings—from the Star Chamber to the Table. In 1577 a controversy between Sir John Zouche and Sir Thomas Stanhope was ordered to be removed from the Star Chamber after the witnesses had been examined, to be heard and finally determined by their Lordships at the Council Table.[3]

Dr. Tanner has stated that in 1570 the Star Chamber had become sufficiently separated from the Council to be regarded as a rival Court.[4] He bases this on a rebuke by the Privy Council to Sir William Paulet, who had complained to the Privy Council against one John Yonge, and had been told to put in writing what he had to say against him. Paulet had thereupon lodged his written complaint not before the Council Table, but in the Star Chamber. The Council wrote to him that "they cannot but find this manner of dealing very strange, and think that he hath therein much forgotten himself; like as they mean not to suffer the authority of this Table to be so much prejudiced as to endure that any matter of complaint brought and dealt by them should by the complainant himself be removed to any other Court before the same be heard by their Lordships and ordered, so he is required with all speed to exhibit his said bill of complaint to the intent the said Mr. Yonge may answer thereto."

It seems that Sir William Paulet thought that the order to prepare a bill, the ordinary method of initiating proceedings in the Star Chamber by private persons, meant that his complaint would be

[1] *Acts of the Privy Council*, 1581–2, p. 271.
[2] *Acts of the Privy Council*, 1618–19, p. 268.
[3] *Acts of the Privy Council*, 1577–8, p. 115.
[4] *Tudor Constitutional Documents*, ed. J. R. Tanner, p. 261.

heard there. It is possible that he wished to have his adversary subjected to the disgrace of public trial and relied on the Councillors deputed that term for Star Chamber duties not being the same as those to whom he had complained, but this seems very unlikely. What annoyed their lordships was that he seemed to have taken upon himself to decide the venue of the trial. They were seised of the case, and had not made up their minds about it. It is true that the Council in the Star Chamber was a different manifestation of conciliar power from the Council at the Table, but it was not and never could have been 'a rival court'.

The same type of error is manifest in Dr. Tanner's description of the Order in Council concerning Printers as a "Star Chamber Decree".[1] There was no such thing as a "Star Chamber Decree". He seems to have been misled by the fact that those members of Council deputed to deal with the censorship of books sat for the purpose in the room known as the Star Chamber. It is true that the wording of the proclamation loosely describes them as "sitting in this honourable Court". The use of the word 'Court' which has many meanings, has often given rise to misunderstandings. Here it must mean the Court Room, not the assembly of members of the Council and Judges. No judges were present. The meeting was presided over by the Archbishop of Canterbury, not by the Chancellor. The room was used for purposes other than that of holding public trials. It was the scene of the Chancellor's address to the judges before they proceeded on circuit, but that address represented the views of the King, or Queen, and the Council, not those of the Council and Judges in the Star Chamber. It was also used for the assay of precious metals, but the resulting coinage was not known as 'Star Chamber money', though, if it had been sufficiently debased, it might have been in later days loosely so described by the enemies of the prerogative.

In brief, after 1540 the King's Council in the Star Chamber was simply a public court which sat for about twelve weeks in all in a year. It is not known (at least to the writer) when judicial proceedings there were made open to the public. It seems possible that this innovation was due to Wolsey, who desired the world to know what happened to certain types of offender, particularly great men who had for long been regarded as practically immune from punishment. In the absence of newspapers of any sort, a public trial

---

[1] *Tudor Constitutional Documents*, ed. J. R. Tanner, p. 279.

was the best way of influencing public opinion, especially when conducted with ceremonious formality by "as it were, the majesty of the whole Realm."[1] The disgrace was also naturally much feared by persons of high standing. Sir John Smyth wrote to Lord Burghley in 1597 begging that he might be tried, and if found guilty, punished, by the Privy Council, and not forced to submit to the shame of a public audience in the Star Chamber.[2] But the Council in the Star Chamber was in fact far less arbitrary than the Council Table. In fact, it was not arbitrary at all, and seems as a rule, though often extremely harsh, to have been eminently fair. The procedure, certainly from Elizabeth's reign, if not before, was as follows. In cases initiated by bill or petition, the attendance of the defendant was procured and he was given a copy of the charges against him, and eight days in which to answer them. He was allowed Counsel. If his answer, which he made on oath, was deemed to be sufficient, he was discharged, and given his costs. If there were doubts about it, he was subjected to examination by previously prepared interrogatories, which again he had to answer on oath. He was not given time to consider, but the questions were read over to him one by one, and he had to reply at once. If a question of fact emerged which seemed better triable at Common Law, an issue was prepared and sent for trial to one of the Common Law Courts, which in due course certified the verdict of the jury into the Star Chamber. After the interrogatories, the plaintiff could, if he wished, put in a 'replication' or answer to the defendant's case. In later times this was not very frequently done. Witnesses, if any, were then examined, either in the Court by the examiner (a clerk) or by commission in the locality concerned. The record of the case being then completed—entirely by the Clerk of the Court or his deputy— it was read to the Court, which also heard Counsel. Each member of the Court in turn gave his sentence, the most junior member first, as in a court martial, and the most senior, the Chancellor or Lord Keeper, or in their absence the Treasurer, last. The decision was that of the majority, the presiding officer having a casting vote.

When the Crown initiated proceedings, the Attorney-General could lay a written information, in which case the person from whom he obtained it could not be produced as a witness. Thereafter proceedings were the same as when initiated by bill. He might,

---

[1] Sir Thomas Smith, *De Republica Anglorum*, ed. L. Aston, 1900, Book III, CIV.
[2] *Calendar of State Papers Domestic*, Elizabeth, 1595-7, p. 421.

however, proceed by *ore tenus*. *Ore tenus* proceedings were much more summary, and were used when the Attorney-General had, or thought he had, strong reasons for believing the accused to be guilty. The accused person was arrested and examined. If he confessed, he was immediately produced before the Court and his confession read, whereon the Court convicted him *ex ore suo* and sentence was at once pronounced. This summary form of procedure was apt to be abused, especially in cases which had a political tinge. It was fair enough if the confession was genuine, but in some cases the court was apt to act on admissions, or what appeared to be admissions, wrung from the accused by the craft of the examiner. Apart from abuse of the *ore tenus* procedure, and, until finally checked, the length and involved complexity of the interrogatories, there is little doubt that a trial in the Star Chamber was fairer than one at Common Law.

Judges never sat as such in the Privy Council. In the Star Chamber they did, and there is no doubt that their presence was beneficial. The Chief Justices of the King's Bench and Common Pleas, or in their absence, two Puisne Judges, or the Chief Baron of the Exchequer, or Barons of the Exchequer, and very occasionally, when no one of higher judicial rank was available, a Master of Requests, were invariably present in later Tudor and in Stuart times. It is not possible to say when they first began to sit. Miss Scofield considered that the two Chief Justices' position as standing members of the tribunal was due not to their being Privy Councillors, but to 3 Henry VII, C. 1—the 'Star Chamber' Act.[1] It was not, however, an emanation from that stillborn measure. The Judges frequently did not attend during the reign of Henry VII. There is no proof that they ever did in Yorkist times, but the desirability of imparting a respectable judicial colour to the proceedings of the Council, when sitting as a judicial tribunal, was recognized as early as the reign of Henry VI, and in earlier times the Chief Justices had always been prominent members of the King's Council for all purposes. The following is among the Articles agreed to in Parliament in 1426. "Item, for as much as it is lykly that many mateirs shall be treted afore the Counsaille, the which toucheth the Kyng's prerogatyve, and Frehold on that oo partie, and other of his subgittes on that other, in which matieres the Counsaille is not lerned to keep the Kynge's right and the parties both, withouten the advis of the

[1] Cora L. Scofield, *Study of the Court of Star Chamber*, Chicago 1900, p. 42.

Kynge's Justices, which been lerned both in his Prerogatives and in his Common Lawe, that in all such matieres his juges be called thereto, and their advis, with their names also, to be entered on Recorde what and how they determyne and advyse therynne."[1] Mr. W. P. Baildon thought that the summoning of judicial officers other than the two Chief Justices to sit in the Star Chamber was first authorized by the inevitable 3 Henry VII, C. 1,[2] but there seems to be no need to attribute their presence to anything else than a desire to make the public administration of justice by the Council as fair and legal looking as possible. Also the fact that the sessions in the Star Chamber were held only in term-time made it impossible for the Chief Justices always to attend.

After Wolsey, the Chancellors were almost always Common Lawyers. Mary reverted to ecclesiastics, but apart from that reactionary interlude, the only non-lawyer heads of the legal hierarchy down to the end of the period were Hatton, a layman (1587–91) and Williams, a Bishop, from 1621 to 1625. The dominant position of the Common Lawyers naturally influenced the procedure of the Conciliar Courts, especially that of the Star Chamber, where the Common Law was represented not only by the presiding officer, but also by two Judges, by the Attorney-General, who conducted all cases for the Crown, and also by all the 'Counsellors' or advocates practising in the Court.

It is therefore perhaps surprising to find that no objection was raised to the hearing of numerous cases in the Star Chamber where there was no question of 'too-great might on one side and unmight on the other', which could have been tried in the Common Law Courts, either at Common Law, or, at any rate since the earlier part of Elizabeth's reign, under statute. As late as 1613 a pronouncement on the extent of the royal prerogative in penal justice was made by the Attorney-General and accepted by members of the Council including the Lord Chief Justice of the Common Pleas, and the Lord Chief Baron of the Exchequer. One James Whitelocke, a Common Lawyer, who three years before had distinguished himself by his attack on the prerogative in the great debate on the legality of impositions, "had affirmed that the King cannot, neither by com-

[1] Outline of the History of the Court of Star Chamber, John Bruce, *Archaelogia*, Vol. XXV, 1834.
[2] *Les Reportes del Cases in Camera Stellata 1593–1609*, ed. W. P. Baildon, privately printed 1894.

mission nor in his own person meddle with the bodies, goods, or lands of his subjects but only by indictment, arraignment and trial, or by legal proceeding, in his Ordinary Courts of Justice, laying for his ground the Statute of Magna Carta: *nullus liber homo capietur* etc., which position, in that general and indefinite manner, was set forth by His Majesty's Council to be not only grossly erroneous and contrary to the rule of law, but dangerous and tending to the dissolving of government. First, for that *Lex Terrae*, mentioned in the said Statute is not to be understood only of proceedings in the Ordinary Courts of Justice, but that His Majesty's prerogative and his absolute power incident to his sovereignty is also *Lex Terrae*, and is invested and exercised by the lawe of the land and is part thereof. And it was thereupon observed and urged that the opinion broached by the said Whitelocke did manifestly (by consequence) overthrow the King's martial power, and the authority of the Council Table, and the force of His Majesty's proclamations and other actions and directions of State and policy, applied to the necessity of times and occasions, which fall not many times within the remedies of ordinary justice, nor cannot be tied to the formalities of a legal proceeding *propter tarda legum auxilia.*"[1]

This is a clear and straightforward exposition of the King's position as regards the administration of justice in cases where the interests of the common weal were affected, and where the ordinary law was too vague and muddled for the Ordinary Courts to be able to function speedily, certainly, and efficiently, or where it was non existent, as in the case of many royal proclamations, particularly those designed to meet some temporary or passing emergency; and there is no doubt that it was accepted by the Common Lawyers, at least until 1641.

By the latter part of Elizabeth's reign crimes of violence committed by persons in high society were much less frequent than they had been, except in Wales and the Marches, and the old-fashioned type of maintenance less common. The giving of livery and retention of retainers had altogether ceased to be regarded. But what had been rare offences, or at least more rarely noticed, had become something of a menace to society—offences involving deceit and fraudulent dealing. Much of the time of the Council in the Star Chamber was taken up with these, especially forgery, perjury, and fraud. All of them were undoubtedly punishable at Common Law,

[1] *Acts of the Privy Council,* 1613–14, p. 211.

and the first two by Statute as well, but their treatment in the
Common Law Courts was extremely restricted and uncertain, and
had apparently been rendered more so by the judicial interpretation
of statutes passed in the reign of Elizabeth. Hudson says, that after
the passing of the Statute of 5 Elizabeth, it became doubtful what
types of forgery were punishable.[1] As an example, he quotes
Manning's case when it was held that the adding of clauses to the
will of a dying man without his knowledge was not forgery within
the Statute.[2] As regards perjury, no one could be punished under
5 Elizabeth C. 9 unless he had actually given false evidence in
court as a witness. Parties to a case were not liable, nor anyone
making a false affidavit. Even a witness was not chargeable with
perjury unless his statement bore directly on the matter in issue.
Hudson gives a detailed examination of what types of false swearing
were punishable in the Ordinary Courts, and which were not, or
were not likely to be. What emerges is that the outcome of a trial
for perjury in the Common Law Courts would be highly uncertain.[3]
As regards fraud "though the Common Law of England hath ever
more abhorred covin and deceit", its treatment in the courts was
also vague and doubtful, especially after the passing of the
Statute 13 Elizabeth C. 5, the proviso to which "that false deeds
made bona fide shall not be construed within the law to be
fraudulent, hath begotten more fraud than former ages ever heard
of."[4]

Libel was also frequently dealt with in the Star Chamber. This,
apart from *Scandalum Magnatum*, was not a Common Law offence,
but up till the breach with Rome had been dealt with entirely by the
ecclesiastical courts, and continued to be within their purview for
long afterwards, indeed up till the end of the eighteenth century.
The ecclesiastical courts, however, were generally ineffective and
could not award damages.

Another class of offence often before the Council in the Star
Chamber included conspiracy, and false accusation. Conspiracy
was punishable at Common Law, but false accusation by one person
was not indictable.[5]

[1] W. Hudson, Treatise on the Court of Star Chamber, *Collectanea Juridica*, London
1792, Vol. II, p. 53.
[2] Hudson, op. cit., p. 70.
[3] Hudson, op. cit., pp. 71–6.
[4] Hudson, op. cit., p. 96.
[5] Hudson, op. cit., p. 104.

In brief, the operation of the Council in the Star Chamber was not restricted either by Common Law or Statute. Hudson sums up the position very clearly when he describes "the great and high jurisdiction of this Court, which, by the arm of sovereignty, punished errors creeping into the commonwealth, which otherwise might prove dangerous and infectious diseases, or giveth life to the execution of laws, or the performance of such things as are necessary in the commonwealth, yea, although no positive law or continued custom of Common Law giveth warrant to it."[1]

Where the Common Lawyers made their influence felt was in the introduction of a measure of legal formality into the proceedings.[2] If a charge was made by bill or petition, as always in cases between party and party, nothing would be considered by the Court, which was not consistent with the allegations made. In a case of maintenance, Bayneham versus Sir T. Lucas 1603, the accusation in the bill was that the defendant had procured jurors to give a corrupt verdict. It was held to be maintenance if any person wrote to jurors simply to appear in any case in which he himself was not concerned, but though this offence was clearly proved, the defendant was acquitted because he had not been charged with it.[3] Also "he that shall be charged in this Court must be charged in his true name; for if John be charged in the Bill, Thomas cannot be punished, although he made answer." Common Law practice is clearly discernible here.[4]

If a person was charged with an offence under a Statute, he was liable to the punishment laid down in the Statute, but the Statute had to be expressly invoked in the Bill.

On the motion of Sir Edward Coke, then Queen's Attorney, it was held that a defendant refusing to answer the bill against him was not to be held as having confessed his guilt; but he would be if he refused to answer the interrogatories which the plaintiff should then draw up.[5]

Counsel were directed to keep strictly to the point.[6] Demurrers, for insufficiency either of matter or form, were frowned upon, as

---

[1] Hudson, op. cit., p. 107.
[2] Hudson, op. cit., p. 6.
[3] Les Reportes del Cases in Camera Stellata, 1593–1609, ed. W. P. Baildon, 1894, p. 165.
[4] W. P. Baildon, op. cit., p. 165.
[5] Hudson, op. cit., p. 155.
[6] W. P. Baildon, op. cit., p. 87.

being put forward almost invariably for the purpose of delaying the case.[1]

Causes in which the plaintiff was not ready on the day fixed for hearing were dismissed, and persons putting in bills which were found 'insufficient' had to pay the defendant costs. False accusations were often dealt with very severely. Lawyers guilty of misconduct were often punished, both for misfeasances in the Star Chamber and those committed in other courts. One Wheatcroft, an Attorney at the Common Bench, was fined £300, sentenced to be hurled over the Bar at Westminster, declared unfit ever to be an attorney again, or to have any office in the law, to be expelled for ever from 'Furnifolle's Inn', and to wear papers describing his offence both at Westminster and at the Assizes in his home county.[2] This was for unfairly obtaining judgment and execution in the King's Bench. An attorney named Irenman, who had forged the sheriff's signature on a writ of *venire facias* (having lost the original) and had altered a panel of jurors, was fined £200, imprisoned, ordered to wear papers in Westminster Hall, and to be debarred from all practice as an attorney.[3]

But the clerks were not supervised, and as in all the courts, effected a working alliance with attorneys, and with the new class of legal practitioner, solicitors. Much trouble was caused by the delegation of duties to the clerk, who being First Clerk of the King's Council, soon grew too big for his boots, and appointed deputies, who did the work for him. Bacon said that the Clerk's place was worth £2,000 a year (the salary was £26 13s. 4d.) and eventually succeeded in getting it for himself. His predecessor, Mills, who held the post for many years, was for long in trouble over charges of extortion, but in the end nothing was done to him. In the time of Henry VII and Henry VIII the Chancellor himself, or one of the judges, used to take the examinations of the parties and draw up the interrogatories. Later the Clerk of the Court was entrusted with this duty, and he handed it on to his underpaid deputies. The results were deplorable. As Hudson said "it lieth in the power of the examiners to acquite the defender and condemn the innocent, yea and to perplex the court by uncertain testimonies, or tire them with frivolous discourse, if that officer be either corrupt or ignorant."[4]

---

[1] W. P. Baildon, op. cit., p. 87.
[2] W. P. Baildon, op. cit., p. 71.
[3] W. P. Baildon, op. cit., p. 80.
[4] Hudson, op. cit., p. 38.

As the work of the court increased the Clerk appointed more deputies, which led Hudson to express the fear that fees would be multiplied and the records of the court mislaid.[1] His forebodings were amply justified.

The spinning out of interrogatories to an intolerable length, partly due to the lawyers' desire "to make contrarieties, which may easily happen to simple men", partly to increase the clerk's copying fees, became a crying scandal and was not finally checked till Bacon's time, by an order which limited the articles to fifteen, of not more than two questions each, any excess to be paid for by the plaintiff, at the rate of fifteen shillings an article.[2] There had been frequent complaints before, especially during Elizabeth's last decade. In 1596, Mr. Justice Wameslowe (Walmsley), a Baron of the Exchequer, went so far as to say that the costs of the interminable depositions would exceed four subsidies, or the finding of twenty horses duly equipped for war.[3]

The Court had ceased to be remarkable for cheapness—nor was its administration of justice as expeditious as it had been. The canker of subordinates' corruption, to which no effective remedy was ever applied, was spreading, even into the King's Council itself, and by the last years of Elizabeth was beginning to militate against the undoubted popularity of Star Chamber justice.

[1] Hudson, op. cit., p. 41.
[2] Hudson, op. cit., p. 170.
[3] W. P. Baildon, op. cit., p. 54.

CHAPTER XV

THE KING'S COUNCIL AND THE CIVIL LAW

THE deterioration of the Court of Chancery inevitably reacted on the Privy Council. Designed to give the ruler and his advisers relief from the task of righting the inequity of the Common Law, by the end of the sixteenth century it was itself providing grievances which could be remedied only by that body. Meanwhile the Common Law continued in its accustomed course—that "Grand Cheat and Abominable Idoll Call'd the Course of ye Courts".[1] The application of the Court of Requests was limited, and it too was tending to abandon expeditious methods. As a result much of the time of the Council, even when most occupied with affairs of the greatest national importance, was taken up in listening to petitions from private persons, either those already ruined by the protraction of suits at law, including many for whom the transference of their case from the Common Law Courts to Chancery was simply the final calamity, or those whose lack of means precluded their attempting to obtain their rights by litigation, even in the Court of Requests. These began to be frequent soon after the accession of Elizabeth, and became steadily more and more numerous during the reign of James I. The petitions abound in phrases such as "being fallen into extreme poverty, and wanting means to recover her rights by the circular and accustomed course of law"; "the petitioner is unable to run the circuit of the law"; "his estate is so weak as he is not able to undergo the charges of suits in law". Such cases, and those in which the petitioner had been the victim of legal chicanery and unconscionable dealing were always regarded as deserving the attention of the Privy Council, even when the nation was locked in mortal combat with the power of Spain. It also frequently tried to settle all sorts of private controversies, especially those arising from the succession to property or disputed marriage settlements, in order to save the parties the possibly ruinous expense attendant upon a law

[1] John Cook to the Lord Deputy, 1655. (Appendix O of *Ireland in the Seventeenth Century* by E. MacLysaght, 1950.)

suit. Sometimes the Council would send the Court concerned an order to expedite proceedings. One of the many reminders to the Chancery after the death of Sir Christopher Hatton, who left many arrears, stated that the tenants of the Manor of Ingleton in Yorkshire had been involved in a suit which had already lasted ten years at law, and four in Chancery, and urged instant expedition, as the unfortunate men were too impoverished to continue the struggle. This was on February 7, 1592. Another letter ordering speedy dispatch was sent on May 26.[1]

Sometimes the Council suggested arbitration, or took the case out of the hands of the courts and appointed arbitrators themselves. As a specimen, in 1579 the judges of Assize in the County of Norfolk were asked to examine the case out of court, or appoint some impartial persons to do so, with a view to settling it, as the petitioner was too poor to seek redress at Common Law.[2] Another in 1593 dealt with a petition by one Alice Bradbury, daughter of T. Sackvile, gent, sometime Groom Porter to King Henry VIII, regarding some lands—"some of which, after three years continuance of the suit, was ready to receive tryall at the Common Lawe by *nisi prius*, which one Elmes, who had a mortgage on them, to prevent and delay proceedings therin procured the cause to be removed into the Chancery, thinking thereby to weary the parties in following the suite."[3] Their lordships referred this case to the Masters of Requests with orders to endeavour to settle it. The Chief Justices themselves were on at least one occasion nominated as arbitrators to avoid a trial at Common Law. In 1577 their lordships addressed George Chaworth Esq. over a controversy between him and one T. Shippman, concerning which they had been approached by one Richard Alvey "a Godly preacher", as Shippman "without his utter undoing is not able to abide the long suit of lawe for the trial of his interest in the case." They therefore desired him to nominate the two Chief Justices as arbitrators, or to choose the one he liked best, and some other person.[4]

There is no doubt that the Council found the burden of these constant petitions well-nigh intolerable. In 1582 an order was passed that no private causes which could be heard in the ordinary

[1] *Acts of the Privy Council*, 1591–2, p. 235.
[2] *Acts of the Privy Council*, 1578–80, p. 59.
[3] *Acts of the Privy Council*, 1591–2, p. 235.
[4] *Acts of the Privy Council*, 1577–8, p. 59.

courts should be submitted to the Council, unless they concerned the preservation of the peace, or were of some public consequence.[1] It was entirely ineffective. The tide of complaints and petitions continued unabated. Seven years later an order signed by eight of the chief members of the Council—The Archbishop of Canterbury, Hatton, Burghley, Warwick, Howard, Hunsdon, Cobham and Buckhurst, laid down that in future the Council would not interfere in suits which could be determined in the ordinary courts. But they found it necessary to allow a loophole. The Council was not to be precluded from reviewing the decisions of the courts in cases of wrong, wilful delay, or denial of justice by any judge or judges in any court.[2] This order gave no relief at all, and two years later the Council attempted to shift the burden on to the Masters of Requests, who were ordered to examine all petitions, and direct the parties to the Courts of Common Law or of Chancery, where such causes were properly triable.[3] The Masters of Requests failed completely, and the Council continued to be as much harassed as ever by attempts to avoid or short-circuit the course of the law, and remained so till the end. The fact was that many people were being denied justice or were being ruined in trying to get it, and that the King was bound to intervene. This he could do, and did, through the agency of his Council acting in his name, but not through the Masters of Requests, who, though sworn of the Privy Council, were really only professional civil judges of not very high degree, and lacked the prestige necessary to deal with Chief Justices and the like. This was apparently realized and the Council expected them to function merely as a post office back to the ordinary courts, which amounted in effect to a denial of justice, and it was found that the order was not enforceable. The feasibility of any attempt to reform the law had long been abandoned. Since 1535 any such idea had been politically impracticable, and the Council was irrevocably condemned, while the personal exercise of the royal prerogative was still possible, to do the best it could by tinkering with individual cases of hardship.

One class of case the Council did attempt to deal with as a whole by executive action, and delegation of its authority to a Commission. The law of debt was remarkable for its harshness. No provision existed for the relief of the insolvent debtor. He could not

[1] *Acts of the Privy Council*, 1581–2, p. 395.
[2] *Acts of the Privy Council*, 1589, p. 181.
[3] *Acts of the Privy Council*, 1591, p. 240.

be released from the gaol to which he had been consigned as, by the
law, the release of his person meant automatically the discharge of his
liability. He was therefore condemned to what in many, perhaps
most, cases was perpetual imprisonment without support of any
kind. His creditor was under no obligation to feed him, nor was the
State. The Fleet, which was the chief debtors' prison, though others
were used for the purpose, Ludgate, the Counter, and also local
gaols, was a dreadful place for those who really were insolvent and
could not pay exorbitant sums to the Warden (whose post was a
hereditary freehold which could be, and was, bought and sold) for
their maintenance. The Beggars' Ward was filthy and verminous
and there the pauper bankrupt was left to his fate, dependent
entirely on such charity as was forthcoming from the outside world.
Many died of starvation and neglect.[1]

The expansion of trade and commerce which gave increased
opportunities to some, brought disaster to others. Foreign wars
particularly the struggle with Spain were responsible for many
bankruptcies. Robbery and piracy were a constant risk. Suretyship
led to the ruin of many. Lawsuits and legal chicanery accounted for
more failures. The Council attempted to mitigate the severity of the
law as regards debtors in many individual cases, and eventually
appointed Commissions to deal with creditors. They were instructed
to induce creditors either to modify the rigour of their demands,
or to allow reasonable time for payment before consigning the
debtor to prison. The Commissioners were directed to threaten
proceedings before the Council Table to those creditors who were
obstinately unyielding.[2] Contempt of a royal command enabled the
Council to take action in cases not punishable by law. The Commissioners themselves were also empowered to commit to prison
creditors who remained obdurate. This led to considerable trouble,
including actions at the Common Law for false imprisonment, and
in one case a letter was issued to three of the Commissioners, who
were having difficulty with some intractable creditors, informing
them that Her Majesty's Commission laid down that any six
commissioners, including always the Archbishop of Canterbury,
were empowered to commit to prison, and that they should be
careful to observe this. Apparently it was thought that the judges
would hesitate to listen to complaints against the doings of the

[1] *The Oeconomy of the Fleet*, ed. A. Jessop, Camden Society, 1879.
[2] *Acts of the Privy Council*, 1589, p. 292.

Archbishop. This however proved to be unavailing, and the Commissioners were then authorized to hold out threats to ruthless creditors as to the treatment they might expect if ever they were to find themselves accused of any other offence before the Council Table.[1] The judges were asked to show no favour to merciless creditors, and not to support them against the actions of the Debt Commissioners.[2] It is clear from this that the Council anticipated further actions at Common Law against the doings of the Debt Commissioners. Their surmise was not unjustified.

There was no chance of obtaining any relaxation of the harsh and stupid law of debt in Parliament, which alone could change the law, as the wealthier commercial classes, represented very fully in the House of Commons, were opposed to any change. The action of the Council undoubtedly did afford relief in a number of cases, but the rigour of the law remained unmitigated for nearly three hundred years. What the exercise of the royal prerogative could do within the limitations imposed by the ideas of the period, it did, but here, as always, the vested interests or accepted policy of the upper classes, or of an influential section of them, were too strong for the application of anything but palliatives.

[1] *Acts of the Privy Council*, 1590–1, p. 9.
[2] *Acts of the Privy Council*, 1591–2, pp. 384–6.

CHAPTER XVI

THE COMMON LAWYER'S COUNTER ATTACK ON CHANCERY AND THE PREROGATIVE COURTS

No sooner was the terrible Henry dead than the Common Lawyers plucked up courage to petition the Council of Regency against the encroachments of the Chancery. In the course of a lengthy supplication by 'divers students of the Common Lawes of this Realm to the Lord Protector and others of the Privy Council', complaint was made that the Chancery had frequently intervened in the course of the Courts, and set aside their orders by decrees based upon the Civil Law, and framed in accordance with the conscience of the individual concerned. The Civil Law, they said, was not binding on the people of England, nor were decrees grounded upon the dictates of conscience and not on certain rule of law.[1] They went on to protest against the grant by the overworked Chancellor of a Commission to the Master of the Rolls and certain Masters of Chancery to dispose of all pending cases. The legality of this Commission was referred to the judges, who held that the Chancellor (the Earl of Southampton) had forfeited his office, and was liable to fine and imprisonment. With this finding the Council who were obviously anxious to placate the Common Lawyers and their allies, agreed, and the Chancellor was deprived of the Great Seal, interned in his house and fined, for misuse of the Great Seal and for conduct tending to 'the great prejudice and utter decaye of the Common Lawes of this realm'.[2] The feeling animating the petitioners appears to have been that the exercise of equitable justice to mitigate the rigours of the Common Law was wholly unnecessary, and that in any case the Chancellor was not empowered to delegate authority and so enable himself to cope with the rapidly increasing business of his Court. Much the same jealousy of Chancery was shown in the slightly earlier tract ostensibly written by 'a serjeant at the law of England',

---

[1] *Acts of the Privy Council*, 1547–50, p. 48.
[2] *Acts of the Privy Council*, 1547–50, p. 56.

who stated clearly that there was no need for the exercise of conscience, as the Common Law was a manifestation of the law of God, and therefore sufficient.[1] Later, however, the Common Lawyers seem generally to have come round to the view that the equitable jurisdiction of the Chancellor was supplemental to the Common Law, as Christopher St. Germain had insisted, and not its rival, and that it could be tolerated so long as it kept within certain limits. Though Civilians continued for long to be appointed as Masters in Chancery, practice in the Court was the monopoly of the Common Lawyers, and those who pleaded there found it most lucrative. The quarrel therefore eventually partook rather of the nature of a civil war, like that between the Courts of King's Bench and Common Pleas after the Restoration. The judges of the Common Law Courts, however, thought that they alone should be entitled to issue prohibitions, and strongly disliked interference in their proceedings by injunctions from the Chancery. Also the vast increase of business in Chancery inevitably caused jealousy, owing to the fact that the whole of the staff of the courts, judges, attorneys and clerks, depended on fees for the whole or part of their emoluments. There was always a tendency in all Courts to try to attract business to themselves.

However, there was no further open outbreak of hostility till Sir Edward Coke became Chief Justice of the Common Pleas in 1606. He did not deny the legality of the Chancellor's equitable jurisdiction, but sought to restrict it to cases which were not triable at Common Law, and also to make the Common Law Courts immune from injunctions. He went so far as to decide that imprisonment for contempt of the Chancellor's injunctions was illegal. This would have been effective because if a Court cannot enforce obedience to its order, it is helpless. In one class of case he attacked the legality of the Chancellor's jurisdiction, strangely enough, on grounds of injustice. Chancery could order specific performance, which the Common Law could not. Coke said that this was unfair as it deprived the defendant of his right to choose whether to pay damages or to fulfil his contract.[2] It had been recognized since the latter part of Elizabeth's reign that the superior remedy provided by Chancery in cases of breach of contract, and still more the fact that the Chancellor could intervene in all cases on grounds of conscience,

---

[1] *Hargrave's Law Tracts*, p. 327.
[2] Cited in Holdsworth's *History of English Law*, Vol. I, p. 461.

even after judgment had been pronouced, was tending to reduce the Common Law Courts to a position of subordination.[1]

It is strange that, so far as the writer is aware, two persons only appear to have seen that the root of the whole trouble lay in the simple fact that law, based on and deducible from writ and precedent, and equity, based on the claims of fair dealing and good conscience, were administered in separate Courts. Henry Brinklow wrote in or about 1542 "Oh Lord, how men be tossed from one Court to another! Yea, and that for smal matters and in manifest and playne causes, even upon a playne obligacyn. Make nor admytt no judge to sit in any Court, onles he be able rightfully to judge any matter or cause that shal be commensed in that Court. And being sufficyent to judge such causes, what shame is it to remove it from that Court to another, as though the King were more stronger or more juster in one Court than another, which surely is nothing but a bucler and defence for the wicked and rych, to prolong delay and to wery him that is in the right. Make no judges therefore (I say) but such as be godly lerned, and able to judge between man and man, and let all things be finished in that Court where thei be begonne."[2] John Cook, who had been a lawyer and judge for thirty-one years, wrote in 1655 to the Lord Deputy of Ireland "Another Grand consideration with me is the distinction of Courts, in the opposing of Law and Equity; whereas poor Ireland (by the blessing of God) hath for four or five years last past tasted of that Great Privilege of placing Law and Equity in the same Courts." He goes on to say "I am sure no man can give any solid reason why any man should be forced to go out of the 'First Court' and further "A Judge, if he be honest and able may cure and remedie every Oppressed Man, no Honest Cause needs to miscarry through any Ignorance or Prevarication of Counsell or Attorney if the Judge be but as Eagle ey'd to find out the truth as any subtile Pleaders can be to conceale it. I say againe, if the judge be able and Honest, it is no great matter what the Councell and Attorneys are, it is but his taking so much the more paines, and though many times the Councell and Attorneys may be Blameworthy enough, yet if the Honest man have not speedie Justice, it is the judge's fault, he must Answer it at the Great Day of Judgement, however he may Pleade Custome in these Inferior Judicatures, and

---

[1] Holdsworth, Vol. I, p. 461.
[2] Henry Brinklow, *Complaint of Roderick Mors*, ed. J. Meadows Cooper, Early English Text Society, London 1874.

his old Plea (that he would help him as a Private man, but cannot do it as a Judge) will be ridiculous at the Last Day. For a Judge ought to have a conscience, as any Private man, and he ought to rectify Erroneous Consciences in a Court of Equity."[1]

What the King and his advisers did see was that the state of the Common Law made frequent interference on grounds of conscience inevitable. Glanville's case in 1615 was a glaring, and decisive, example.[2] Glanville had sold a jewel worth £20 to a gullible young man named Courtney for £350, and also some other jewels for £100, which were apparently worth that sum. He obtained an instalment of the price, and took a bond for the payment of the balance in the name of one Hampton. An action on the bond was in due course brought in Hampton's name, and a surreptitious judgment procured, which was quite easy to do through the collusion of the attorneys concerned. There was no possibility of relief when the real value of the jewellery was discovered, except in Chancery, which in due course issued an injunction against the enforcement of the decree, and ordered Glanville to take back his jewel and £100, and obtain a release and admission of satisfaction from Hampton. Glanville did not obey and was imprisoned. Coke, then Chief Justice of England, declared that this decree and imprisonment were unlawful, being subsequent to a judgment at Common Law. After quoting a case of Edward IV's reign where a decree obtained by collusive confession of an attorney had been upset only by a special Act of Parliament, he went on to maintain that the Chancellor's jurisdiction in cases in which a judgment had issued from a Court of Common Law was contrary to the Statute of Praemunire. Now that Statute was passed to prevent appeals from the King's Courts to any 'foreign' court (meaning the Papal Curia or Ecclesiastical Courts in England drawing their authority from Rome). The word 'foreign' however was not used, but by loose drafting the phrase 'autre cour'. Coke pounced upon this, and said it meant any Court other than those of the Common Law, and that Courtney had committed an offence against the Statute of Praemunire by going from Common Law to Chancery. This was obviously absurd. It shows how far Coke, the high priest of the Common Law, was prepared to go to protect a manifest swindler when the supremacy of the Common Law judgments was at stake. He failed. James, advised by learned

---

[1] John Cook, Letter to the Lord Deputy, Aug. 1655.
[2] *Collectanea Juridica*, Vol. I, pp. 20–2.

counsel, including Francis Bacon, pronounced a final judgment himself on the right of the Chancellor to intervene at any stage of proceedings.[1] This was decisive. Chancery jurisdiction, having survived the attack on the prerogative Courts in 1641, was not again questioned till the days of the Interregnum, apart from an abortive bill brought forward by Coke in the Parliament of 1621, when seizing the opportunity presented by the disgrace of Bacon, he proposed that the Common Law Chief Justices should sit with the Chancellor at all rehearings of Common Law cases.

Great and undeniable as were the hardships and injustices liable to be caused by the rigorous application of Common Law rules, it is certainly arguable that the victory of Chancery was a calamity. Had it lost, the Common Law judges might conceivably have been driven by the rising tide of discontent, particularly among the growing lower middle class, to fill up some of the gaps in their system, to recognize trusts, to develop their immature law of contract, and even to permit the raising of equitable considerations by defendants—in short to combine at least to some extent the administration of legal and equitable justice long before the Judicature Acts of 1873. The spur of the Chancery's competition had already for some time compelled them to develop the offshoots of trespass, particularly actions on the case, and 'ejectment', which last had indeed displaced the ancient and intricate technicalities, both of process and pleading, of the real actions.[2] Furthermore, the determination to secure the great and growing volume of mercantile business had shown that the Common Law could slowly by tortuous and painful elaboration be adapted to cope with a class of business for which it

[1] In the course of it he said—"For as much as mercy and justice be the true supporters of our Royal throne, and that it properly belongeth to us in our princely office to take care and provide that our subjects have equal and indifferent justice ministered unto them; and that where their case deserveth to be relieved in course of equity by suit in our Court of Chancery, they should not be abandoned and exposed to perish under the rigour and extremity of our laws. . . . And do will and command that our Chancellor . . . shall not hereafter desist to give unto our subjects upon their several complaints now or hereafter to be made, such relief in equity (notwithstanding any proceedings at the Common Law against him) as shall stand with the merit and justice of their cause, and with the former and continued practice and presidency of our Chancery." *Collectanea Juridica*, Vol. I, pp. 53–4.

[2] A real action was an action in which the specific thing demanded could be recovered. Such actions were almost entirely limited to interests in land, including incorporeal rights. For the merits of the form of action on the case known as 'ejectment' as compared with the old real actions see Holdsworth, *History of English Law*, Vol. VII, p. 4.

was entirely unfitted, in spite of the seemingly conclusive restrictions of writ and precedent.

The Lord High Admiral had in the fourteenth century acquired jurisdiction in commercial cases, particularly those in which foreign merchants were concerned, and where the cause of action had arisen outside England. No provision for the trial of such cases existed, nor, as it appeared, could ever be made, at Common Law, which was applicable only to this country. This jurisdiction, like that of the Chancellor, appears to have been delegated by the King's Council which had previously exercised it. The judges were Civilians, and the practice of the Court was in the hands of Civil lawyers. The procedure, which was of the conciliar type, had by the sixteenth century been allowed to become dilatory, and the Court required frequent supervision by the Council. The Court had much business, and during Elizabeth's reign the Common Law judges began to covet it. By the middle of the reign they had formulated their plans for the capture of the administration of mercantile law in spite of its alien content. They began to issue Prohibitions to the Admiralty Court, based largely on a most transparent and absurd legal fiction, which enabled the English Common Law to claim jurisdiction over happenings outside England by describing whatever place was concerned as situated 'in the parish of S. Mary le Bow in the Ward of Cheap', and showed itself ready to admit the existence of Merchant Custom, if duly proved in each individual case. Coke in fact declared in 1606 that the Law Merchant was part of the Law of the Realm,[1] by which he meant part of the Common Law. But the task of fitting it into the ancient structure was not an easy one, and the administration of commercial law suffered inevitably as the result of the conflict of jurisdictions. The number of prohibitions and the consequent delays in the settling of mercantile causes grew rapidly at the end of Elizabeth's reign, and the trading classes lost time and money while the Common Law judges were slowly adapting their antique machinery, and at the same time holding up proceedings in the already sufficiently dilatory Court of Admiralty.[2] In 1600, the Council addressed H.M.'s. Council Learned (Mr. Serjeant Yelverton, Mr. Attorney General, Mr. Solicitor, and Mr. Francis Bacon) asking them to confer with the judges on the subject of the constant issue of prohibitions staying proceedings in the

---

[1] T. F. T. Plucknett, *Concise History of the Common Law*, p. 624.
[2] *Acts of the Privy Council*, 1600.

Admiralty Court, which were productive of intolerable delays, and had given rise to many complaints both by the Queen's subjects and those of foreign powers. Diplomatic protests were made by the Spanish Ambassador,[1] but the judges persevered, and the Queen and Council did not feel themselves strong enough to check their encroachments. Finally in 1632 Charles I's Council succeeded in effecting a compromise whereby certain classes of suit were recognized as pertaining exclusively to Admiralty jurisdiction.[2] At the Restoration however the Common Lawyers were able, in this as in all other rival Civil jurisdictions, to establish their supremacy, and by the close of the seventeenth century had succeeded in reducing the Admiralty Court to little more than a name.

The next move was an attack on the legality of the jurisdiction of the Court of Requests. The first prohibitions were issued by the judges of the Common Law Courts in 1590, and in 1599 a writ of habeas corpus was issued for the release of a man imprisoned by the Masters of Requests for contempt, on the ground that 'this which was called a Court of Requests had no power of judicature'. When Sir Edward Coke became Chief Justice of the Common Pleas in 1606, the number of prohibitions rapidly increased, with the object of making the exercise of the Requests jurisdiction impossible.

The Common Lawyers had evolved a theory that to be legal a Court of Law must have been established by ancient Royal Commission, or ordinance; or by Statute; or have existed from time immemorial. The Court of Requests did not seem to fulfil any of these requirements. It had sat regularly only since 1493, and therefore could not claim immemorial custom. To strengthen their position the judges held in 1614 that the Chancery had an absolute monopoly of equitable jurisdiction, and that no new commission or court administering equity could be recognized by the law.

Coke, in supporting the decision of the judges of 1599, denied that the Masters of Requests had originally exercised judicial functions. He wrote in his *Fourth Institute* 'that such petitions as were exhibited to the King and delivered to the Masters of Requests should be perused by them, and the party directed by them to take his remedy, according to their case, either at the Common Law, or in the Court of Chancery.'[3] He may have been right. The persons who originally

---

[1] *S. P. Dom, 1611–18*, p. 146.
[2] *S. P. Dom, 1631–3*, pp. 427, 516, 519.
[3] Coke, *Fourth Institute*. Cited by J. R. Tanner, *Tudor Constitutional Documents*, p. 311.

received the 'requests' of poor people were probably mere sifters of petitions. But he has ignored the fact that poor men's causes were sometimes adjudicated upon by the undifferentiated King's Council, though not by members specially appointed for the purpose, until Yorkist times. Since the middle of the sixteenth century however the abiding place of the Masters of Requests in the White Hall looked exactly like—and indeed was—a regular Court of Law, sitting in term-time like the Courts of Common Law, and presided over by professional judges who had no other function. But the Masters were all sworn of the Privy Council, and so were technically as much entitled to exercise conciliar jurisdiction as any of those who attended at the Council Table. This vital point was ignored by Coke, and all the Common Law Opposition.

It seems that the case put forward by Sir Julius Caesar, the great apologist for the Court, to prove 'that the Court of Whitehall or Requests is a member and parcel of the King's most honourable Council attendant on his person' is unanswerable.[1] There was no constitutional reason why the King should not appoint certain members of his Council for the sole purpose of carrying out regularly and efficiently what was undoubtedly one of his duties. There was nothing to distinguish the age-old jurisdiction of the Council over poor men's causes, in pursuance of the King's sworn duty to do justice to all men, from that of the Court of Requests, except its regularity and the quantity of business with which it dealt.

The Common Lawyers had had no reason to be envious when the cases only of such poor persons as could reach the King on his progresses were heard. They were too few, and as Coke said, many were simply passed on to the ordinary courts. But by the close of the sixteenth century the business of the Court—or Council—of Requests was very considerable indeed, and though little was to be made out of the plaintiffs, the defendants were often men of substance. The Court, together with Council of the North, and Council in Wales and the Marches, was in fact doing on a much larger scale and continuously, the work of the old itinerant justices on the civil side of their duties. It is not too much to say that these Courts had become the Court of Common Pleas for plaintiffs of the poorer

---

[1] "This Court", he said, "is one of the King's Courts and standeth only by prescription of the King's Council, as appeareth by the Acts of this Court and the Common Law, it having neither Commission under the Great Seal or Act of Parliament to establish it otherwise; but the King's Council prescribeth only for itself." See Tanner, *Tudor Constitutional Documents*, p. 308.

classes. But, so long as the jurisdiction of the Court of Requests was limited, as it was supposed to be, to the plaints of persons too poor to allow of their attempting to establish what they believed to be their rights at Common Law, there could be no valid grievance. The King and his advisers could easily have countered the biased researches of the Common Lawyers into the past history of the Masters of Requests. But they did not do so, and for twenty-five years or so the work of the Court was grievously hampered.[1] However the Common Lawyers were not ultimately victorious. After the dismissal of Coke in 1616 the Court began to revive, and in the reign of Charles I flourished exceedingly.

The same reason which was responsible for the attack on the Court of Requests led to attempts to thwart the proceedings of the Council of the North, and of that of Wales and the Marches. Both of these subordinate Councils, but especially that of the North, tended, as something like order was slowly established, to become courts of equitable justice, and particularly of civil justice, rather than administrative and executive bodies. By the end of Elizabeth's reign the Council of the North was hearing nearly eleven hundred civil cases a year. In 1609 Coke wrathfully declared that it had 'above two thousand cases depending at one time, whereas the Chancery, that extends into forty-one English countries and twelve in Wales had in Easter term but ninety-five, and in Trinity term but seventy-two.' He attacked its jurisdiction by means of prohibitions as soon as he succeeded to the Chief Justiceship. The number of these declined after his dismissal, but some continued to be issued, and late in Charles I's reign Wentworth spoke of 'the bleeding evil of prohibitions', which he temporarily cured by ignoring them.[2]

Like the Council of the North, the Council of Wales and the Marches appears to have been popular as a dispenser of equitable civil justice. Both bodies had suffered from the appointment as members of unsuitable persons, and also from the excessive number of attorneys and clerks who found employment under them, which,

---

[1] "Their sittings are not warranted. Their decrees cannot be executed. Their authorities are condemned. Their prisoners are discharged by habeas corpus. Their suitors proceedings are stayed by prohibitions. Their orders scorned and publicly slandered. Themselves unmeasureably toiled without profit, yea, to their great hindrance, and which is most of all subject in the censure of four grave judges to most severe punishment as mad busybodies that sit in places of judgment without warrant of law." Anonymous, c. 1600. Cited J. R. Tanner, op. cit., p. 311.

[2] R. R. Reid, *The Council of the North*.

as always, gave rise to inefficiency and corruption. But in 1594 it was said of the Council of Wales 'Generally it is the very place of refuge for the poore oppressed of this country of Wales to flye unto ... and for this cause it is as generally frequented with suytes as any one Court at Westminster, the more for that it is the beste cheape Court in England for ffees, and there is great speed made in the tryall of all causes.'[1] The gentry, however, particularly of the four border counties of Shropshire, Worcestershire, Herefordshire and Gloucestershire, strongly disliked it, partly no doubt because of the facilities it afforded to their tenants and others to sue them, partly, perhaps, because the fact that they were subject also to the jurisdiction of the Courts at Westminster, caused considerable confusion. The forms of law were abused on occasion by the practice of instituting simultaneous suits in several courts, both in the Marches, and in Westminster, for the settlement of the same dispute, the object being to harass the defendant by the multiplication of legal costs, and the expense of travel. Coke and the judges supported the local gentry by afflicting the Council with prohibitions. James I was apparently under no illusions as to the source of the trouble. In the course of a conference with Coke and the judges in 1608 he said, 'None doe oppose themselves against the jurisdiction of the Councell in the Marches, but certain high headed fellows, calling them by a Scottish name mountinge fellows, in English, swaggering fellows, such as Herbert Crofte and others to the number of three or four, who, because they would oppress the meaner people, and beare the whole sway of their country without controulement doe oppose themselves against government and the State of the King'.[2]

Coke found it a little difficult to allege illegality in the case of either of these Councils. The Council of the North was an ancient Lord's Council taken over by Richard, Duke of Gloucester, when he became Lieutenant of the North, and kept in being by him after he succeeded to the throne, as a subordinate royal Council. It was abolished in 1509, but was reconstituted in 1525, and reorganized after the Pilgrimage of Grace by Henry VIII's Commission. Coke chose to ignore its earlier history, and found an opportunity for attack on the ground that the Commission was not ancient, and also

[1] Dialogue on the Government of Wales, between Barthol, a Doctor of the Civil Law and Demetus, a Pembrokeshire man; by George Owen of Henlys, 1594. Cited C. A. J. Skeel, *The Council in the Marches of Wales*, 1904.
[2] C. A. J. Skeel, *The Council in the Marches of Wales*, Girton College Studies II, 1904.

that until the reign of James I the instructions to the Commissioners were not published.

The Council of Wales and the Marches was doubly legal according to the Common Lawyer's touchstone. It seems to have originated in a Royal Commission, possibly of the reign of Edward IV,[1] but received statutory authority in the reign of Henry VIII (26 Henry VIII C. 6, and 34 and 35 Henry VIII C. 26). But this did not suffice to save it from constant interference, and the hostility of the gentry of the border counties was supported in the Parliamentary Petition of Grievances of 1610. It is noteworthy that Coke's objections—and also those of the House of Commons—were purely legalistic. There was no consideration whatever of the nature of the work which these Councils were doing, or of whether or not it was necessary and beneficial. Also it is to be observed that with the single exception of the judges' differences with the Privy Council in 1593 on the question of committal to custody without trial, for which indeed they appear to have had some justification at the time, the counter attack was limited to jurisdiction in civil matters. One reason was doubtless the determination to maintain the supremacy of the Common Law as the guardian of property. Another was the fact that civil litigation yielded the fees on which judges and practitioners alike depended, and that civil practice in the courts could be immensely lucrative, whereas little was normally to be gained from criminal proceedings, either to judges, advocates, attorneys, or clerks, except in the Star Chamber where wealthy people were frequently involved, and there too the Common Lawyers enjoyed a monopoly of advocacy.[2]

No special sanctity appears to have been attached to Common Law criminal procedure. Coke, in spite of his conviction of the paramount supremacy of the Common Law, wrote of the Star Chamber, in which he had served as Attorney-General and sat as judge 'and seeing the proceeding according to the laws and customs of this realm cannot by one rule of law suffice to punish in every case the exorbitancy and enormity of some great horrible crimes and offences, and especially of great men, this Court dealeth with them to the end that the medecine may be according to the disease, and the punishment according to the offence, *ut poena ad paucos, metus ad omnes perveniet*: without respect of persons, be they public or private, great or small.' His attitude as regards the civil side of the law was

---

[1] C. A. J. Skeel, op. cit., p. 18.

[2] Coke, *Fourth Institute*, cited J. R. Tanner, op. cit., p. 291.

very different. There one rule was sufficient, whatever hardship or injustice might result from its application. But the Star Chamber was 'the most honourable Court (our Parliament excepted) that is in the Christian world, both in respect of the Judges of the Court and of their honourable proceeding according to their just jurisdiction, and the ancient and just orders of the Court . . . and it is truly said *"Curia Camerae Stellatae, si vetustatem spectemus, est antiquissima, si dignitatem honoratissima."* This Court, the right institution and ancient orders thereof being observed, doth keep all England in quiet.'

The alliance of the Common Lawyers with the Puritans was a curious one, but it developed comparatively early, owing to their ancient dislike of the ecclesiastical Courts, the operation of which had been rendered effective by the High Commission. That body, though not technically conciliar, was in fact the ecclesiastical arm of the government, and up to 1583 had been directly under the control of the Council. To it was entrusted the maintenance of the Royal Supremacy over the Church. Without it, as Archbishop Whitgift said, 'the whole ecclesiastical law is a carcass without a Soul.' From 1584 onwards its functions had become largely judicial from having been almost entirely visitatorial. The spiritual penalties formerly imposed—and still the only form of punishment available to the ordinary ecclesiastical courts—had lost their terrors. Obstinate Puritans, and indeed many who were not Puritans, cared little for excommunication. But, by the royal interpretation of § VIII of the Elizabethan Act of Supremacy, the Commission could both fine and imprison, and was therefore able to enforce its decrees.

There is no reason to suppose that the Common Lawyers as a body were opposed to the Royal Supremacy, or that they had any genuine sympathy with those who refused to conform. The inmates of the Inns of Court and Chancery had indeed been suspected of Romish rather than Puritan Nonconformist tendencies in Elizabeth's reign.[1] They were however, acutely interested in suits arising from disputes about the distribution and commutation of tithes. The boundaries between ecclesiastical and Common Law jurisdiction in this matter were vague. In 1591 the judges in Cawdrey's case had declared the High Commission to be a legal court, but from 1606 onwards the judges, led by Coke, issued a stream of prohibitions against its proceedings based on their conception of the meaning of § VIII of the Elizabethan Act of Supremacy. Loose drafting had made

[1] *Acts of the Privy Council*, 1577–8, p. 94.

K

possible the view that Letters Patent issued from time to time to lay
down the duties and powers of the Commission were not restricted
in their content by the terms of the Act itself.[1] The judges held that
the Act had simply transferred control of ecclesiastical jurisdiction to
the Crown, but had not envisaged any alteration of procedure or
penalty. Spiritual punishments alone should be inflicted, save in
cases of heresy or incontinence by priests, where the imposition
of temporal penalties had been authorized by Parliament in Statutes
of the reigns of Henry IV and Henry VIII. Prohibitions were issued
from 1598 onwards, and writs of habeas corpus granted, especially
during Coke's tenure of the Chief Justiceship, on every type of case,
including convictions for simony, heresy, schism and adultery,
although the judges were personally interested only in suits concerning Church property, particularly tithe. But as they could
contest the right of the High Commission to try them only by
impugning the basis of its effective authority, they were compelled
to attack indiscriminately every exercise of the Commission's
powers. In 1610 the Archbishop, Bancroft, succeeded in showing
beyond doubt or cavil the damage that the action of the judges was
doing to the Established Church, and a compromise was effected.
But the hostility simmered on, and the strangely assorted alliance
between the Puritans and nonconformists generally, which seems to
have had its origin in a dispute over property jurisdiction, was firmly
established and became by no means the least of the factors in the
downfall of the monarchy.

It seems that the main motive for the great attack on the Conciliar
Courts which began towards the close of Elizabeth's reign, and was
checked in 1616 by the dismissal of Chief Justice Coke, was at first
merely the determination of the Common Lawyers to establish the
supremacy of their mystery in civil actions, or even to destroy all
other competing jurisdictions, and not dislike or distrust of the royal
prerogative as such, though they were resolved to clip it where it
directly touched their interests. But there had long been signs that
the ancient system based on the royal prerogative of government,
and the absolute right of the subject to his property was breaking
down. The Crown was forced to adopt highly dubious methods of

---

[1] "Such person or persons so to be named, assigned, authorised and appointed by
Your Highness . . . shall have full power and authority, by virtue of this Act and of
the said letters patents . . . to exercise, use and execute all the premises according to
the tenor and effect of the said letters patents; any matter or cause to the contrary in
any wise notwithstanding." Act of Supremacy, § VIII, 1559.

making ends meet, and the Commons now beginning to feel personally interested in the doings of the central government (for which the Reformation and the Royal Supremacy over the Church were largely responsible) had discovered as early as 1566 that the power of the purse was capable of levering the ruler out of undoubted prerogatival positions. After the defeat of the Spanish Armada the majority of the upper classes seem generally to have felt that there was no longer any pressing need for a powerful central government. Fear of internal chaos, and of foreign invasion, had, perhaps prematurely, dwindled, and various sections of dissidents, who for long had nursed their grievances, thought that the time had come to seek remedies and to challenge royal authority.

The country gentry, whose real interests were usually entirely local, resented the interference of the Central Government in their economic affairs, and also the annually recurring demand for subsidies. The trading classes were aggrieved by the constant granting of monopolies to Court favourites and 'projectors', and were backed by a great weight of public opinion. They also became keenly interested in foreign policy—signs of this had been apparent as early as Wolsey's time—and critical of the King's conduct of it, as were the upper classes generally, and especially those of them who were strongly anti-Catholic. The Puritans detested state control of the Church, and desired to advance fast and far on the road of continental Protestantism. The lawyers wished their mystery to be the sole guardian of rights in property. Not until the reign of Charles I did these parties coalesce completely into one temporarily united opposition. Till then the Crown had been engaged in a number of more or less separate campaigns. From early in the reign of James I, however, there had been a strong tendency for the Common Lawyers to become the General Staff of all the dissident forces. They had common interests with all of them, social, political, and economic, and Coke, a host in himself, though not a Puritan, yielded to none in the bitterness of his detestation of Roman Catholicism or anything that savoured of it. They were the traditional guardians of the subject's prerogative, which had become in their hands not merely a guarantee of individual rights in property, but a most potent weapon of political opposition to the personal government of the hardpressed King.

It seems likely that the lawyers' hostility was sharpened by the knowledge that James, used to a different system in Scotland, was no admirer of the Common Law, and that his confidential adviser, Francis Bacon, when Attorney-General, had actually submitted a scheme of law reform to his master.[1] He proposed to cure the existing evils by weeding out all that was obsolete, and then making a digest or codification of the Common Law and also of the Statutes, which contained 'such an accumulation concerning one matter, and they so cross and intricate, as the certainty of law is lost in the heap.' Nothing was done, but James on several occasions showed his sympathy with the project. It may well be that the vindictive bitterness of the attack on Bacon when Chancellor was due in some measure to his attempt to unveil the mysteries of the Common Law.

In a speech to both Houses in 1609, James is reported to have said that he wished that three defects could be removed from the Common Law—the use of Norman French, which enabled the lawyers to keep the people in ignorance of what the law was, as the Romish priests did the Gospel; that case law might be abandoned, and an authoritative codification settled by Act of Parliament, and that statutes which were inconsistent one with another should be reviewed and reconciled. Bacon's influence is clearly perceptible here. He ended by attacking the superfluity of prohibitions 'every court striving to bring most grist to its own mill'.[2] In his speech to the Judges in 1616 he animadverted sharply on 'the vain popular humour of some lawyers at the bar that think they are not eloquent and bold spirited enough except they meddle with the King's prerogative'.[3] According

---

[1] He enumerated the defects as follows—"Certain is that our laws, as they now stand, are subject to great uncertainties and variety of opinions, delays, and evasions; whereof ensueth:

(1) That the multiplicity and length of suits is great.
(2) That the contentious person is armed and the honest subject wearied and oppressed.
(3) That the judge is more absolute; who, in doubtful cases, hath a greater stroke and liberty.
(4) That the Chancery Courts are more filled, the remedy of law being often obscure and doubtful.
(5) That the ignorant lawyer shroudeth his ignorance of law in that doubts are so frequent and many.
(6) That men's assurances of their lands and estates by patents, deeds, wills are often subject to question, and hollow, and many the like inconveniences."

A Proposition to His Majesty by Sir Francis Bacon, H.M.'s Attorney General and one of his Privy Council, touching the compiling and amendment of the law of England. Works, ed. B. Montagu, V, p. 341.

[2] Arthur Wilson, *History of Great Britain, being the Life and Reign of King James I,* London 1653, p. 46.

[3] *Constitutional Documents of James I,* ed. J. R. Tanner, p. 18.

to a pamphlet of 1649—'The corruption and deficiency of the Laws of England soberly discovered'—he also said, possibly on the same occasion, 'In countries where the formality of law hath no place, as in Denmark, all their state is governed only by a written law; there is no advocate or proctor admitted to plead, only the parties themselves plead their own cause, and then a man stands up, and pleads the law, there is an end; for the very law book itself is their only judge. Happy were all kingdoms, if they could be so; but here curious wits, various conceits, different actions, and variety of examples, breed questions in law.'[1] This was highly ominous. According to Simonds D'Ewes the King was overheard to say, after Bacon's surrender of the Great Seal "Now, by my soul, I am pained at the heart where to bestow this; for as to my lawyers, I think they be all knaves."[2] He gave it to Bishop Williams.

It seems probable that the readiness of the lawyers to join and indeed to direct any party of opposition to the prerogative owed something to their consciousness of the marked unfriendliness of James.

[1] *Harleian Miscellany* (ed. of 1809), Vol. II, p. 259.
[2] *Autobiography of Sir Simonds D'Ewes*, Vol. I, p. 188, ed. J. O. Halliwell, 2 vols., London 1845.

CHAPTER XVII

THE DIRECT ATTACK ON THE KING'S GOVERNMENT

THOUGH it may perhaps be too much to say that by the beginning of James's reign the parties of opposition had definitely decided to break the ancient conception of monarchical government, it seems certain that they had come to the conclusion that they should no longer be excluded from the *arcana regni*. Since the middle of Elizabeth's reign the Royal Supremacy over the Church had made a proportion of the educated classes feel more deeply concerned with the doings of the central government than they had before. They were as sensitive in their consciences as they were in their pockets, and the Puritan element, which was much more strongly represented in the House of Commons than in the nation at large, felt that the regulation of religious belief and ceremonial should not be in the hands of the monarch alone. Moreover James's views on religion were already highly suspect, and his openly expressed dislike of Puritanism was by no means offset by his hatred of Jesuits.

Some at least of the dissident factions, first and foremost the Puritans, had come to realize that only in Parliament, with the support of their privilege, could they successfully oppose the King, and indeed seek to encroach upon his undoubted prerogatives by the simple method of withholding supply. But the King and his advisers, notably Salisbury, had discovered a possible way of escape from dependence on Parliament for funds. This was by the levy of impositions. Impositions were additional or enhanced customs duties, nominally for the beneficial regulation of trade, but really as a rule to increase the Crown's hopelessly inadequate revenues. The growth of commerce was such that the power to levy enhanced duties unchecked would provide an opportunity for the Crown to tap the rapidly increasing wealth of the country, and might go far towards reducing the need for summoning parliaments.

The Common Law was silent on the subject of foreign trade, but it was realized that though the levying of impositions for the bona fide regulation of trade was an undoubted royal prerogative, arbitrarily to raise the duties merely to increase the royal revenues was in effect to tax the subject without his consent, and could therefore be held to be directly contrary to Common Law principle. James and Salisbury got round this by interpreting 'pro bono publico' in a general sense. According to them the levy of impositions was justifiable not only as a means of assisting local manufactures or industries, or of restricting the import of undesirable articles, or the export of warlike stores to countries with whom a breach was possible, or in retaliation for excessive duties laid on British goods by a foreign power, but for the general relief of the Crown's necessities. As a rule James was content to theorize vaguely about his absolute prerogative, but in his Commission authorizing the collection of additional imposts, he definitely stated that the levying of customs and impositions on imports and exports was a universally recognized prerogative in order that the King might raise sufficient funds to support his Crown and dignity (provided that trade was not prejudiced thereby).[1] Salisbury also said in a conference shortly before the great debate on impositions that he took it *pro concesso* that the King's just necessity must be relieved by his people, and that the King was governor of his subjects and was not absolutely to depend upon the will of the people in point of subsistence.[2] The claim that the King must have sufficient funds with which to carry on the government was certainly reasonable, and from his point of view, at any rate, it was *pro bono publico* that he should have them. But it was new, and extra-legal. It certainly alarmed the opposition, as did the fact that encouraged by the judgment of Chief Baron Fleming in Bate's case, a general increase had been made in the Book of Rates. Fleming was a strong supporter of the prerogative, and the Exchequer was always more accommodating than the other two Courts.

At this time Coke was organizing the campaign against impositions in the Courts, but the assets of the Common Law, especially as the source of authoritative precedents, had for long been placed at the disposal of the opposition. The leaders in the attack of 1610 were Hakewill and Whitelocke, both Common Lawyers, and both, like Coke, skilled researchers into forgotten statutes and Year Book precedents, which, suitably interpreted, could be made to supply a theoretical and also a historical basis to the demands of the opposition.

[1] Cited in *Statutes & Constitutional Documents 1558–1625*, W. Prothero, Oxford 1898, p. 354.
[2] *Parliamentary Debates 1610*, Camden Society, 1861, p. 151.

Hakewill based his argument in the first place upon the 'certainty' always stressed by the Common Lawyers as the great beauty of their mystery. The King therefore could not be allowed to raise money arbitrarily and to any extent he pleased by means of impositions. He therefore deduced the position "That the Common Law giveth to the King no perpetual revenue or matter or profit out of the interest or property of the subject, but it either limiteth a certainty therein at the first, or otherwise hath so provided that if it be uncertain in itself, it is reduceable to a certainty only by a legal course, that is to say, either by Parliament or by judge and jury; and not by the King's own absolute will and pleasure." He went on to deny what had always formerly been allowed, that the King could levy taxes without the assent of Parliament on the occasion of a grave and sudden emergency, and pointed out that the acceptance of this would give away the whole position, as no one was judge of emergencies but the King.[1] He clearly foresaw the possibility of the hard-pressed King turning his sole discretion in this matter to practical account, which Charles I later did in the case of Ship Money. Such action, however, apart from its being in accordance with the Coronation Oath, was certainly justifiable at Common Law. A man would not be liable for damages if he broke down a farmer's fence to prevent someone from being gored to death by a bull. Nor could the King, in the event of a sudden invasion, be accused of breaking the law, if he took some of his subjects' property in order to prevent their losing it all. But Hakewill did not trust James, and he wished to weaken the absolute prerogative of the Crown even in the discharge of the King's primary duty, and to assert and strengthen that of the subject. He therefore urged that the law had provided for any sudden emergency by invasion by allowing compulsory military service by every subject at his own charges on any such occasion. But property the King must not presume to touch. "If it were otherwise you see how it were to the utter dissolution and destruction of that politic frame and constitution of this Common-wealth which I have opened unto you, and of that excellent wise providence of the Common Law for the preserving of property and the avoidance of oppression."[2]

Whitelocke's arguments were more general and, in addition to stating the illegality of impositions without consent, amounted to

[1] *Constitutional Documents of James I, 1603–25*, ed. J. R. Tanner, p. 250.
[2] *Constitutional Documents of James I, 1603–25*, ed. J. R. Tanner, p. 253.

nothing less than a claim for the sovereignty of Parliament. "The sovereign power", he said, "is agreed to be in the King: but in the King is a twofold power—the one in Parliament, as he is assisted with the consent of the whole State; the other out of Parliament, as he is sole and singular, guided merely by his own will. And if of these two powers in the King, one is greater than the other, and can direct and control the other, that is suprema potestas, the sovereign power, and the other is subordinata. It will then be easily proved that the power of the King in Parliament is greater than his power out of Parliament, and doth rule and control it." No final decision was reached as the result of the debate of 1610, as James dissolved Parliament before a bargain could be completed. None the less it definitely marked a stage in the uneven battle between royal prerogative and subject right, and clearly showed that the ancient dichotomy had ceased to be a workable system.

Outside Parliament the two Chief Justices, Popham and Coke, had given their opinion that the King could not levy impositions at his pleasure 'save for the advancement of trade and traffic.' This view was not justifiable historically, but the times and conditions had changed since the reign of King John, and was certainly true in 1610, in spite of unchallenged Tudor precedents to the contrary.[1]

The superiority of the King in Parliament over the King alone or in Council was also claimed during the same year, 1610, in the attack on Proclamations. Such legislation as there was prior to the latter part of the thirteenth century had been almost entirely by proclamation or ordinance by the King in Council. Before the days of Parliament proclamations had been the sole source of what was later called legislation. Not until the fourteenth century were statutes passed by the authority of Parliament. But though the King in Parliament had then been regarded as the source of measures of a permanent nature, the King in Council had never abandoned his legislative powers, though they were progressively restricted to executive orders of a more or less temporary nature (which, if necessary might subsequently be made permanent by statute), or to the sphere of the royal prerogative, where the liberties of the subject did not have to be considered, such as foreign affairs, including trade, military service, and the coinage. The King in Council had been forbidden by the King in Parliament to issue proclamations touching freehold or a franchise, and an attempt had been made to debar him

---

[1] *Constitutional Documents of James I, 1603–25*, ed. J. R. Tanner, p. 264.

from inflicting capital punishment or mutilation. He had not accepted this disqualification, but in practice almost always observed it.   Otherwise no firm line was drawn between the provinces of statute and proclamation.   The Common Lawyers had, however, by James's time evolved, or rather assumed, the theory that when once statute entered a field, any other occupant necessarily withdrew. James, by failing to observe the prohibition regarding freehold (he had ordered the pulling down of houses in London) gave them the opportunity to challenge the legislative authority of the King in Council.   Elizabeth had several times ignored the limitations on her proclaiming power, and had issued proclamations imposing the death penalty on idlers and vagrants, and on rescuers of prisoners, which, though legal, was a breach of long established convention, and also on building houses in London, which was illegal, as freehold was or might be concerned.   Mary, too, in 1558 issued a proclamation denouncing the penalties of martial law for the possession of a treasonable book.[1]   No objection had been taken in any of these cases, but the times were changed when James succeeded.   A vigorous protest against his use of proclamations was made in the petition of Grievances in 1610, as having been extended 'not only to the liberty, but also to the goods, inheritances and livelihood of men', which roused a fear that a new form of arbitrary government was in course of preparation.[2]   James replied that he realized that proclamations were not of equal force with laws, but that they were necessary in emergencies, when no Parliament happened to be sitting, and promised to issue no more which were not compatible with existing law, or covered by precedent.   Precedent was almost certainly on James's side, and he could have fought the lawyer politicians on their own chosen ground with every chance of success, but he and his advisers apparently shrank from the labour of research. The Chief Justices were asked for their views, and Coke, who was followed by his colleagues on the Bench, gave as his opinion that the King could not create new offences, nor punish them in the Star Chamber.   He also laid down a ruling that the law was divided into three parts, Common Law, Statute Law, and Custom, and that the King's proclamation was none of them.[3]   This was manifestly untrue. The enforcement of royal proclamations was certainly customary

---

[1] R. R. Steele, *Catalogue of Tudor and Stuart Proclamations,* Vol. I, p. LXXXV.
[2] *Constitutional Documents of James I, 1603–25,* J. R. Tanner, p. 154.
[3] *Constitutional Documents of James I, 1603–25,* J. R. Tanner, p. 188.

and was, indeed, older than the Common Law, though Coke would not have admitted that. Finally he said that 'the King hath no prerogative but that which the law of the land (by which he apparently meant the Common Law) allows him.' Here again an extra-judicial decision by the judges was used to support the political opposition. The practical point which they were trying to establish was that disobedience to proclamations should not be punished by fine or imprisonment. But contempt of the royal authority had always been punishable, and offenders could still be dealt with for that, though not sentenced to undergo fixed penalties for doing what they had actually done. For the next ten years or so very few proclamations did fix penalties, but referred to the King's displeasure and such punishments as might legally be imposed. The King had not been driven off the ground, but his position had definitely been worsened by the unrebutted assertion that the law was not on his side.

The next move against the King's Government yielded unexpectedly decisive results. It was directed in the first place against certain monopolists. Unlike the attack on impositions it was not a frontal assault on the royal prerogative, and was concerned not with the law on the subject, but with facts. The law had nothing to say about monopolies. During its formative period the regulation of trade, domestic as well as foreign, had been exclusively a royal prerogative, and the right of the King to advance local industries or encourage inventions by the grant of a monopoly was difficult to counter by purely legal argument. It could not be said that the general public were in effect being taxed, as no claim had ever been put forward that such grants could be made merely to increase the revenues of the Crown. The judge of whether or no the public would be benefited was the ruler, and the assertion that it would be benefited was not traversable. But in practice the grant of monopolies had for some time been made with the merest verbal pretence of 'pro bono publico'. Elizabeth was forced by extreme financial stringency to use her prerogative in this matter to reward or pay her servants, and to compensate needy courtiers. James had carried on the practice which since 1597 had been a crying scandal.

The Commons could not bring themselves to provide the Crown with sufficient funds to meet the day-to-day charges of government, which would have obviated the necessity of its adopting such deplorable expedients. Instead they endeavoured to compel the

Crown to give them up, without cost to themselves. In this they received the aid of the lawyers. The debate of 1601 should have been a sufficient indication that the way to remedy the evil was to attack individual grants, and show that they had resulted in extortion and oppression, and constituted a public grievance. Coke, however, was determined to prove that monopolies, at least of the kind usually granted, were illegal, and made a valiant attempt to extract yet another type of 'new corn from the old fields'. He was thrown back on Magna Carta, and appeals to Statute Law, which required much ingenious misrepresentation, and also on the Year Books, in the effort to show that these grants were contrary to Common Law principle. In reporting the great case of Darcy v. Allin he quoted a precedent of the time of Edward IV to prove that letters patent granting a charter of office to a person were void if that person were not capable of discharging it. Darcy held a monopoly of the manufacture and import of playing cards. He was a Groom of the Queen's Privy Chamber, and entirely unskilled in 'the mechanical trade of making cards'. But the patent made provision for the employment of factors and deputies. Coke got round this by inventing a maxim which he used as though it embodied a known principle of the Common Law—'If the grantee himself is inexpert, and the grant void so far as he is concerned, he cannot make a deputy to take his place, "quia quod per me non possum, nec per alium".' Magna Carta was made to do duty on the ground that monopolies were against the liberty and freedom of the subject, and therefore against the law of the land. By the time he wrote his *Third Institute* he had discovered various other precedents, notably Peachie's case of 50 Edward III, which he deliberately misinterpreted. Peachie had enjoyed a monopoly of the import of sweet wines into London, and had lost his grant, not because the patent was invalid as being monopolistic, but because he had been extortionate. Coke was trying to establish a new Common Law principle asserting freedom of enterprise, and to demonstrate that it was not new at all, but deducible from the decisions of the past. The case is a good example of the way in which unscrupulous interpretation of the 'incognoscible' Common Law could be used—in this instance to counter a dishonest use of the prerogative, and curtail a manifest abuse.[1] The attempt was not successful, but it helped to make the Common Lawyers appear

[1] See Coke and the Rise of Economic Liberalism. D. O. Wagner, *Economic History Review*, 1935.

in the light of protectors or at least would-be protectors of trade and of the interests of both producer and consumer, as well as of property. They had already been prominent in the great debate on monopolies in 1601, when Hakewill of Lincoln's Inn, the forerunner of Coke, and later one of the leaders in the debate on impositions, asked whether bread was not included in the list.

In 1621 the effort to win the victory on a point of law was dropped. A lawyer named Noy, who later turned Royalist, and is credited with the invention of Ship Money as a fiscal device, moved for a Parliamentary inquiry into the grant of monopolies, which had become more scandalous than ever. He drew attention to the fact that these patents had been referred for examination and report, before they were granted, to a Committee including the Chancellor (Bacon) and the Treasurer and proposed that they should be sent for and examined. His motion was seconded by Coke, now a Member of Parliament. There is no doubt that the monopolies which had attracted their attention were not only useless to the public, but positively noxious and oppressive in the extreme, especially the patent for the regulation of inns, which was held by the notorious Sir Giles Mompesson, and which he had used simply for barefaced wholesale extortion. It seemed clear that an inquiry would not only reveal gross negligence, if no worse, on the part of the two ministers, but also that the mighty Buckingham, under whose patronage Mompesson had perpetrated his enormities, would almost certainly be involved. The resurrection of the ancient weapon of impeachment, unused since the fifteenth century, was then almost a necessary conclusion, and for the first time for a hundred and fifty years it would be possible for the opposition effectively to challenge the basis upon which the 'new monarchy' rested—the responsibility of the King's Council to the King alone. In brief, it seemed that the 'new monarchy' might be endangered, and the Lancastrian position restored, with the vital difference that the control of the central Government would pass not to a handful of magnates, but to the majority party in the House of Commons, aided by such of the lords as chose to agree with it. For the moment, however, the Commons hesitated, and the lawyers had to be content with a dress rehearsal. Mompesson was impeached and convicted in his absence, and the facilitation of his villainy by the King's great ministers was passed over in silence. But the effectiveness of the revived procedure of impeachment by the Commons and judgment by the Lords had been proved, and the ill feeling against the ministers concerned, especially Bacon, the Chancellor, remained. Complaints of gross dishonesty in the office of the Chancery, and of corruption by the Chancellor himself, readily provided another opportunity, which was taken. The charges against Bacon were admittedly true, but he had in fact done nothing that his predecessors (and the Common Law Judges) had not always done regularly (if slightly more carefully), and with impunity. James, doubtless advised by Buckingham, who presumably hoped that the sacrifice of a scapegoat would divert the wrath of Lords and Commons from himself, made only feeble efforts to save him. Bacon's conviction was a deadly blow. The implications of their success were fully realized by the leaders of opposition, and in 1624 Coke and Sandys laid before the Peers the Commons' charges against Cranfield, James's financial saviour. The impeachment was favoured by Buckingham who feared Cranfield's hostility to the policy of war with Spain. So, when the old King died, Charles found himself facing the triumphant 'inquisitors-general of the grievances of the Kingdom', with only Buckingham, the architect of ruin, to support him.

To sum up, the counter attack by the Common Lawyers, which had begun as an independent campaign against conciliar jurisdiction in civil causes, had developed into the support and even the leadership of opposition to the exercise of the royal prerogative of government. The Common Law had come to be regarded as the champion of 'popular' rights against the Crown, and Cowell, the author of the 'Interpreter' had been violently attacked for speaking of it disrespectfully, as well as for indicating that the prerogative, which on occasion invoked the use of discretionary power, could not always be limited by law. The assault was checked, though not defeated by the dismissal of Coke from the Chief Justiceship of the Court of King's Bench in 1616, which gave the sorely battered 'new monarchy' a short breathing space. But he and others, notably Hakewill, continued constantly to assert the sovereignty of the Common Law as being the frame of the constitution and the guardian of subject right. Their vigorous revivification of mediaeval theory had enabled them in the changed conditions of the seventeenth century to use it as a potent weapon of offence against the ancient kingship. Researches into long forgotten precedents and their interpretation in the light of present political needs, had enabled the revolutionary party to pose as the champions of time-honoured rights. From henceforward the King and his Council, already forced on to the defensive, had to reckon on the prestige of the Common Law and the abilities of its professors being permanently at the disposal of the growing party of opposition. As Dr. Tanner has said 'The first dismissal of a judge for reasons that were in the main political, is a landmark in constitutional history.'[1] Coke, as the events of 1621 had shown, was far more dangerous in the House of Commons than he had been on the Bench.

[1] *Constitutional Documents of James I, 1603–25*, ed. J. R. Tanner, p. 176.

CHAPTER XVIII

THE KING'S COUNTER ATTACK ON THE COMMON LAW, AND ITS DEFEAT

THE alliance between the Common Lawyers and the Parliamentary opposition had been largely consolidated by the election of Coke to the Parliament of 1621. From the accession of Charles I, if not slightly before, the alliance became a complete fusion.

Coke had an unrivalled knowledge of ancient statutes and could pick and choose among them at his will. He was also the most eminent Year Book specialist of his time, and could always find—or, if necessary, invent—precedents to support his views. Once it was admitted that there was a fundamental law, vague but supreme, crystallized in part in Magna Carta (which document Coke had disinterred from comparative obscurity) and distillable as to the rest from the ancient decisions of long forgotten judges, it was clear that it could be authoritatively declared and interpreted only by those steeped in antiquarian legal learning, and of these Coke was the exemplar. The King had no Year Book specialists to take his part. He doubtless could have had, and might have used their researches to counter fairly and honestly the often misleading assertions of his antagonists, but foolishly or neglectfully allowed to the opposition the practical monopoly of the use and interpretation of precedent; so though he had the preponderance of history and tradition on his side, his enemies were usually enabled to claim that the past was on theirs, and that he was the innovator. This in view of the innate conservatism of most educated Englishmen, and of the need they almost felt for theoretical justification by precedent, gave the opposition an ultimately decisive advantage, in that they could manoeuvre without effective challenge or interruption, and go forward to make claims which, however reasonable in the light of the existing circumstances, were in fact revolutionary, in the guise of assertion of ancient right.

Charles and his advisers did however perceive that the rigid distinction in the Common Law between questions of law and questions of fact might enable him to debar his opponents from raising the real issue, however illegal and tyrannical his actions might be.

In 1626 he was in the most acute financial difficulties. He had been unable to obtain adequate funds from Parliament for the prosecution of the war with Spain, highly popular though it was, partly owing to the dislike and distrust with which his incompetent minister and favourite was justly regarded, partly because of doubts as to what his war policy was (he had never explained it) and partly because of unwillingness to pay the high cost of military operations on the Continent. What the Parliament men wanted was a cheap naval war—which might indeed be marginally remunerative—attacks on the Spanish Plate fleets and buccaneering exploits after the manner of Drake. But Charles had already entered into heavy commitments to his allies, and had rashly taken Parliamentary approval for granted. In desperation he fell back on the deplorable expedient of a forced loan, and dismissed Lord Chief Justice Crew because he would not certify it to be legal. Seventy-six rich men, who refused to lend, were imprisoned or interned. Five of them sued out a writ of habeas corpus. To this the customary return in cases of a political nature was made—that they had been committed 'per speciale mandatum domini regis'. This gave away nothing. No mention was made of the fact that they had been imprisoned for declining to lend the King money. When therefore the case was argued before the judges, the prisoners' counsel were restricted to the point of law—whether imprisonment by the King's command without the reasons therefor being stated was legal or not. The best they could do was to plead Magna Carta. No free man can be imprisoned except by "legale judicium parium suorum vel per legem terrae". But, whatever may have been the meaning of this much disputed clause, it was certain that the King had always had, and also that he must have, power to commit to prison, and that the words 'per speciale mandatum domini regis', due and sufficient reason being necessarily taken for granted, put the case outside the power of intervention by the courts. Looked at from a strictly legal point of view, the writ of 'habeas corpus cum causa' is a command from the King to some authority or court to show why it had put someone in prison, and it was obviously absurd to expect that he should show cause to himself why he had done so. Moreover, though there are a number of mentions of Magna Carta in the Year Books and Plea

L

Rolls of the later Middle Ages, they all occur in cases between party and party. It had apparently never been used in any way against the King. His power to commit for 'reasons of State' had never been challenged. It was however clearly necessary to endeavour to produce a counterblast to Charles's discovery that he could use his undoubted and necessary prerogative as a screen behind which he could freely mulct his subjects. The only possibility which occurred to the opposition was to try to prove that he had no such prerogative, and Cap. 29 of Magna Carta was therefore pressed into service. Coke and Selden, both of whom knew better, seem to have been mainly responsible. Not only was the whole of past history, and the unchanging necessity of every Government, ignored, but also existing conciliar procedure. Coke, who had had nothing but good to say of the Star Chamber, in which he had served for many years, adopted for political purposes the theory that the Common Law only was the law of the land, and that every free man was entitled to the benefits of its procedure (laid down as he apparently believed, or affected to believe, in Magna Carta) as his indefeasible birthright. He went so far as to declare in the Commons that "the King can arrest no man, because there is no remedy against him". He must act through the judges. In the course of a conference with the Lords he stated that "To be a tenant at will for liberty he could not agree to; it was a tenure could not be found in all Littleton."(!)[1]

The Court, however, could not ignore the past, and Chief Justice Hyde summed up by saying that the precedents were all against the prisoners' case, and that where no cause of commitment was expressed, it must be presumed to be matter of State, which was outside the competence of the courts.[2] The decision was good law. The facts were not in issue. But its effects were mischievous. The King was encouraged to use his legal prerogative in an unfair way in order to break the stranglehold of subject right on his financial resources. The opposition were convinced that the King could not be trusted, and that their personal liberty, as well as their property, was at his mercy.

The result of their embitterment was the Petition of Right, which the King was eventually compelled to accept. But though Coke himself drew it up, it was not at all well drafted. Magna Carta,

---

[1] Lords' Journals, III, pp. 761–2. See also Faith Thompson, *Magna Carta*, University of Minnesota Press, 1948, p. 342.

[2] *Constitutional Documents of the Puritan Revolution*, Gardiner, 3rd ed., p. 64.

Coke's 'King Charles's head' had a prominent place in the argument, in spite of its obvious irrelevance and its rejection by the judges in the Five Knights' Case only six months before. Forced loans were indeed declared unlawful (which they were), but there was nothing in the Petition (wrongly termed 'the great Statute' by Gardiner) to prevent Charles from saying that 'per speciale mandatum domini regis' was cause shown, that committal with that sanction only was according to the law of the land, and that an answer to a Petition could not alter the law, but merely affirm it. The Lords—and at the time the King also—did not realize this, and proposed the insertion of a clause designed to leave the King free to use in emergencies what was obviously a necessary sovereign power. The lawyers in the Commons at once objected, and Coke in particular rebelled against the word 'sovereign' being applied to the royal power. "I know", he said, "that prerogative is part of the law, but 'sovereign power' is no Parliamentary word. In my opinion it weakens Magna Carta and all our Statutes, for they are absolute, without any saving of 'sovereign power', and shall we now add to it, we shall weaken the foundation of law, and then the building must needs fall. Take heed what we yield unto: Magna Carta is such a fellow that he will have no 'sovereign'." The fact that an argument so clearly contrary to law could be adduced by so great and experienced a legal luminary as Coke shows how completely the Common Lawyers' hostility to the prerogative courts had merged in the general political opposition to the King's Government. The fact is that the King, though dishonest in fact, was right in law, but the opposition could not bring themselves to admit this, and so were forced to fall back upon fallacious argument and patent misinterpretation. The events leading up to and out of the Five Knights' Case provide an illuminating picture of the difficulties of both the King's Government and the opposition, and of the methods to which each was driven in the attempt to solve them.

Charles learnt little from his partial defeat over the Five Knights' Case, or from the tempest of ill feeling which his unblushing use of legal chicane had aroused. Seven years later the levying of Ship Money provided an even more glaring example of dishonest use of a correct decision by the judges on a point of law to provide a transparent legal veneer to an arbitrary and 'unconstitutional' course of action.

There were many precedents for the commandeering of ships for the protection of the country in an emergency, and one (in 1619) for the assessment of the ports in money instead of in actual vessels. It was, however, felt that the towns and counties which directly benefited by sea-borne traffic should alone contribute—an example of the prevailing local rather than national feeling. And, when ships were taken, and not cash in lieu, it was only ports which could supply them. In 1635 Charles extended his demands for Ship Money to the whole kingdom, and a good deal of discontent, and even passive resistance, was aroused. Charles therefore decided to ask the judges, who could be called upon to act as legal advisers to the Crown, whether the extension of his demand to the whole country was legal. Ten of them replied that it was, when the whole country was in danger, of which the King was the sole judge. Judge Croke did not sign the document, but did admit that the charge should be borne by all when the whole country's safety was concerned. Judge Hutton also did not sign it. In 1637 resistance to the levy had become serious, and Charles decided to strengthen his position by another more detailed extra judicial decision by the judges, to whom he put the following question—"When the good and safety of the kingdom in general is concerned, and the whole kingdom in danger, whether may not the King, by writ under the Great Seal of England, command all the subjects of our kingdom at their charge to provide and furnish such a number of ships, with men, victuals, and munition, and for such time as we shall think fit, for the defence and safeguard of the kingdom from such danger and peril, and by law compel the doing thereof, in case of refusal or refractoriness; and whether in such a case is not the King the sole judge of the danger, and when and how the same is to be prevented and avoided?"[1]

This time the judges unanimously replied that the King could so command all his subjects, and that he was the sole judge both of the danger, and when and how it was to be prevented. Charles then decided in effect that there was an emergency justifying the general levy of Ship Money, and that there would be one every year till further notice.

It has been said that the King's case had no merits, and that it was based upon an ingenious conspiracy to tax the country without Parliamentary approval. The second part of this charge was undoubtedly true, but something can perhaps be said in partial justification of Charles's deliberately *mala fide* reliance on the letter of the

[1] *Constitutional Documents of the Puritan Revolution*, Gardiner, 3rd ed., p. 108.

law, which was undoubtedly on his side. In the first place was there an emergency? There was certainly no sudden emergency which called for instant action without waiting to summon a Parliament. But in the sense that there was an emergent need to improve the navy, there was. One of the charges against Buckingham in 1626 had been that as Lord High Admiral he was responsible for the deplorable conditions in the English Channel, where piracy, not only by Dunkirk sea robbers, but by Muhammadan rovers from Algiers and Sallee, had almost brought trade to a standstill. But Oliver St. John made an unanswerable point in his argument in Hampden's case when he showed that the writs were issued seven months before the ships were wanted, and that therefore there would have been ample time for summoning a Parliament. There was, however, no guarantee, or even likelihood, that the money would have been forthcoming. Charles had ruled for eight years without a Parliament, and thanks to the fact that after the death of Buckingham he had been advised, at least on domestic affairs, by able, industrious, and honest men, notably Laud, Wentworth, and Juxon, he had been able to carry on very successfully as far as the internal government of the country was concerned, with the aid of financial expedients of varying degrees of legality. The masses were generally content, but the politically valid class, who feared the King's encroachments on their rights of property, strongly disliked his religious policy, and were justly indignant at his futile and vacillating conduct of foreign affairs, were not. All Charles could expect from Parliament was a string of grievances, and a violent assault on the royal prerogative. Subsidies, however genuinely and urgently required, would not have been voted, except at a price which he, believing devoutly as he did in his divine mission as King, was not prepared to pay. He did spend the funds he raised from the collection of Ship Money, or at least a considerable proportion of them, on the rehabilitation of the navy, and it was in part at least due to the Ship Money Fleet that the naval supremacy of England was achieved in the time of the Common-wealth and Protectorate. Pepys stated in Parliament in 1677 that the victories in the Dutch war were due, not to superiority of numbers but to the great ships built by Charles I, whose superior gun power had done the real business against Tromp.[1]

It seems just possible that the judges failed to observe that the

[1] Heads of a Discourse in Parliament on the business of the Navy. Pepysian MSS. Miscellanies II, pp. 453–9. (Pepys Library, Magdalene College, Cambridge.)

words used by Charles—'to command all the subjects of the kingdom at their charge to provide and furnish ships . . .' undoubtedly
could be held to cover the levying of taxation for the purpose, or the
demand of money in lieu from those who did not possess ships, or
did not own those of the specified size. Perhaps they thought that
non-shipowners were to furnish the ships with crews, victuals and
munitions. It is perhaps unlikely, but Judge Croke, who signed the
answer to Charles's question in 1637, reverted to Hakewill's line of
1610 and held, when Hampden was tried for refusing to pay his
assessment, that though the King might in emergency order his
subjects to attend him, and also commandeer their ships, he could
not levy a charge to provide new ships. Indeed, in Hampden's case,
only seven of the twelve judges decided in favour of the King, in
spite of their unanimously favourable reply to his query.

Charles's victory had been due to his recognition that the rigid
division in the Common Law between questions of law and questions
of fact could be turned to his advantage as readily in the Ship Money
affair as in the Five Knights' Case. There is no doubt that this
dichotomy has its merits.[1] But if the King could gain a decision,
affirmed by all the Common Law judges, on the point of law that in
certain circumstances his prerogative was absolute, and that he only
could determine when those circumstances had arisen, and alone
could decide when and for how long to use it, then the facts did not
matter in the least. If he said there was an emergency, that was
conclusive, even though it was clear that in fact there was none.
He could do as he pleased, and was enabled to use his victory on the
question of principle actually to levy taxation for as long as he chose
without consent in time of peace, with the appearance of the Common
Law of England being behind him. Charles had stated that he intended to keep the ships 'for such time as we shall think fit'. But he
had no intention of handing over the ships built out of Ship Money
to the subscribers, when the emergency was past, or of paying back
the money. 'Such time as we shall think fit' might mean 'for ever' if
he chose. This was naturally infuriating to the opposition, and not
least to the lawyers, who seem to have failed to observe the danger to

---

[1] "Half the confusions of thought in the world, not excepting the world of political
discussion, have arisen because men have not stopped to ask themselves whether the
issue they are debating is one of fact or of principle. 'Do I deny the facts, or do I
dispute the inference?' Or, in legal words, ought I to plead or to demur?" James
Bryce, Development of the Common Law, *Law Quarterly Review*, 1908, Vol. XXIV,
p. 18.

which the 'popular' cause was exposed by the sharpness of the separation of issues of law from issues of fact, when the royal prerogative of government was the subject of debate. It is indeed highly questionable whether the view put forward by Croke and the other dissenting judges in Hampden's case in their effort to save something out of the wreck of subject right, was legally sound. In the last resort all depended on the *bona fides* of the King.

Charles, however, stood to lose far more than he had gained. The upper classes were more than ever exasperated by the knowledge that chicane could give the King's government at least a semblance of legal cover in its attack on the prerogative of the subject.

It seems likely that next to the enforcement of Laudian ideas of uniformity in religion, the audacious use of the Common Law itself to make a bridge between royal prerogative and subject right was the most potent cause of the almost unanimous hostility to Charles's government which was manifest among the politically minded classes in 1640, though the lawyers themselves appear not to have understood how it had been possible. When defeat in the second 'Bishops' War' caused the royal financial system to break down, and made the calling of the Long Parliament unavoidable, the House of Commons, with strong support from the Lords, was determined not only to put an end to Charles's arbitrary personal government, but also to ensure that nothing like it would ever happen again. The Common Lawyers played the leading part. The orginal members of the Long Parliament included seventy-five barristers, all of whom supported the opposition until the battle between the Common Law and the prerogative had been won. It seems that with one exception —Gray's Inn—the Inns of Court had not become anti-Royalist, or even thoroughly anti-Stuart. Up to August 1641 there had been unanimity, but after that date many lawyers, including Hyde, sided with the King—thirty-three as against forty-two for the opposition. When elections to fill vacancies took place, thirty-three more lawyers found seats, and naturally enough in the then existing circumstances, all of them were more or less anti-Royalist. Gray's Inn, in particular, seems to have been for long a nursery of discontent with the Stuart régime, and perhaps even of republicanism. Pym, the leader of the opposition, was a Middle Temple man, but the majority of Charles's most thorough going enemies among the Common Lawyers both in the House and outside it came from Gray's Inn. They included Sir Arthur Hazelrig, Denzil Hollis,

John Bradshaw, Sir Thomas Fairfax (less thoroughgoing than some)
General Lambert, George Fleetwood, Admiral Deane, a number of
Cromwell's relations, and more than a third of the regicides. The
Rump Parliament contained no less than forty-six Gray's Inn men,[1]
about twice as many as the representatives of any of the other Inns.
No reason can at present be adduced for the fact that Gray's Inn was
a focus of revolutionary sentiment, and a study of the careers of its
Benchers and Readers from about 1590 to 1640 has not supplied a
clue.

In the early stages of the Long Parliament, the sanctity of the
'fundamental law' was generally relied upon, as being pre-eminently
the guardian of property rights, to repel the usurpations of the royal
prerogative under cover of 'reason of state'. They were so thoroughly
permeated by Coke's revival of the mediaeval idea of sovereignty,
that they could not realize that the law could be turned to the victory
of the executive in the sacred field of private property, and they were
inclined not to blame the King for dishonest interpretation, but the
judges for having given a false judgment. Magna Carta, they
believed, was a sure shield, and the judges should have sheltered
behind it. Pym, at the opening of the Parliament had mentioned
among the grievances to be remedied 'the extra judicial declarations
of judges, without hearing of counsel or argument'. Not least
among the many strange developments manifested in the words and
actions of the Long Parliament was the rapid widening of the rift in
the ranks of the legal profession, the barrister members of Parliament
versus the Bench. It had begun in 1629, when Charles determined to
punish Eliot and the others responsible for resisting the order to
adjourn the House, and the judges appeared to be lukewarm in
countering the King's manoeuvres. It was clear that they were not
prepared to accept the opposition's view of the position of the House,
which seems to have been that anything which the House of
Commons did or wished to do was covered by privilege. Charles
had indeed succeeded in taming the judges to a considerable extent.
He had the great advantage of appointment to the Bench, and had
made the best use he could of it. Also he had not hesitated to dismiss
Chief Justice Crew, and had suspended Walter, the Chief Baron of
the Exchequer. Possibly too the judges had come to the conclusion
that the House of Commons might become a more formidable

[1] See D. Brunton and D. H. Pemberton, *Members of the Long Parliament*, 1953,
pp. 5, 26 and 46.

opponent of the judicial freedom of the Bench than the King. Certainly during the 'Eleven Years tyranny' a number of Common Lawyers, presumably largely in the hope of professional advancement, had turned to the side of the King from that of the 'popular' party, which could no longer help them after the cessation of sessions of Parliament. The outstanding example is Noy, who had taken a prominent part in Parliamentary opposition to the King's government, but who is believed to have suggested the extension of Ship Money to the King. Among the judges, Judge Berkeley, though he may not have been a thoroughgoing absolutist, stated in the King's Bench, when Chambers appealed to it in 1636 in regard to his fine and imprisonment for refusal to pay Tonnage and Poundage, that "there was a rule of law and a rule of government, and many things which might not be done by the rule of law might be done by the rule of government". When the Long Parliament met, so high did feelings run that trained and experienced Common Lawyers could violently attack a probably correct legal judgment (that on Hampden's Case) because of the political advantage it had given to the executive, or rather, enabled the executive to take. The fact that they were themselves establishing the superiority of a political decision to one based on the law of the land was obscured to them by the general and persistent belief that Parliament was primarily a Court, the highest Court in the Realm, and that its decisions were judgments designed to declare the law or to clarify it, or to bring it up to date. The idea that a sovereign legislature could override the law as it pleased, and even repeal Magna Carta itself, did not however dawn until the power of the King's Government had been crippled.

"The Judges' Judgment, a Speech, penned in the Beginning of Parliament, against the judges, *per ignotum quemdam*" clearly expresses the views of the lawyer-led opposition at the time. "He that well weighs this little word, property, or propriety in our estates, will find it of a large extent; the leeches that have sucked this blood have been excise, benevolences, loans, impositions, military taxes, ship money, *cum multis aliis* all of which spring from one root." This root he considered to be the extra-judicial answer of the judges to Charles's question, which 'unless it were grubbed up' would lead to the general annihilation and confiscation of property, as on the pretence of danger the King could take what, when, and where he willed. He accused the judges of having made the King's subjects mere tenants at will of their liberties and estates, and went so far as to recommend their execution.[1]

Lord Keeper Finch, who had been Chief Justice of the Common Pleas at the time of the Ship Money decision, was impeached, and a commission of inquiry was appointed to examine the conduct of the other judges. The levy of Ship Money was declared to be illegal, and the Act abolishing it laid down that 'the extra judicial opinion of the said Justices and Barons . . . and the said judgment given against the said John Hampden were and are contrary to and against the laws and statutes of this realm, the right of property, and the liberty of the subjects.'[2]

None of the opposition foresaw that barely more than a year later the logic of events would have forced them to adopt the very standpoint against which they had fought so vehemently—that *salus populi* was *suprema lex*; that 'Reason of State was something more sublime and imperial than law'; that the actions of Parliament should be guided not primarily by law, but by interest of state 'for what can particular acts of law, which are to increase our private and domestic profit, advantage us when it is doubtful in so great dangers whether we may enjoy our lives at all, or no?'[3] It had become clear that an ordinance passed by a bare majority of the members of the two Houses would take the wall of Magna Carta. None could foresee that Cromwell would be able without reproach openly to admit doing what Charles had ventured to do only under cover of a legal subterfuge. "And though some may think it is a hard thing," he said in 1655, "without Parliamentary consent to raise money upon this nation: yet I have another argument . . . whether they prefer the having of their will, though it be their destruction, rather than comply with things of necessity? That will excuse me . . . and the people . . . will not be so angry but they will prefer their safety to their passions, and their real security to forms, when necessity calls for supplies."[4] No dog barked.

The ancient notion, so strongly revivified by Coke, of an underlying and unalterable fundamental law had received a mortal wound, though it took an unconscionable time to die. Indeed its faint ghost still occasionally reappears. The Levellers endeavoured to bring it

[1] The Judges' Judgment, *Harleian Miscellany* (ed. of 1808 et seq.) Vol. V, p. 493.
[2] *Constitutional Documents of the Puritan Revolution*, Gardiner, 3rd ed., p. 191.
[3] Henry Parker, *Animadversions adnimadverted*, 1641.
[4] *Oliver Cromwell's Letters and Speeches*, ed. Abbott, Vol. III, p. 89.

back to full vigour in order to protect what they considered to be the natural rights of freeborn Englishmen from the tyranny of their representatives, and to make government tolerable by ruling out its operation from certain spheres. But the ideas of Henry Parker, the Long Parliament propagandist (strangely enough a Common Lawyer) on unhampered Parliamentary sovereignty were ultimately to triumph absolutely. In brief, the paradoxical result of the victory of the lawyer-led opposition over the personal government of the King was that in the fulness of time subject right would have invariably to give way not only to emergent measures in time of danger or apprehended danger, but to legislation expressly designed to alter the 'propriety of estates' in order to bring about great social and economic changes. The transference of executive power to the majority party in the House of Commons, foreshadowed by the defeat of the King's Government in 1641, meant the eventual disappearance of the power and prestige of the Common Law as the subject's champion against the encroachments of Government. The whole nation was held to be represented by a bare majority in Parliament, and could do what it liked with its own. While the wealthier classes monopolized political representation, that consequence of the revolution could not be foreseen, but the growing demands of the middle classes, and later, the organization of labour, made electoral reform inevitable. In 1832 it began to be realized by the upper classes for the first time that the fences round freehold were threatened. In 1867, when the great Whig Party committed suicide, it was clear that they were in grave danger of coming down altogether.

Having led the assault on the inherent power of the King to levy taxation in emergencies, the lawyers proceeded to direct the attack on the prerogative Courts, which had made personal rule possible by the enforcement of proclamations and the punishment of those who had offended against the orders of government, though not against Common or Statute Law. The objectives were the judicial authority of the King's Council at the Council Table, and also in the Star Chamber, the Council of the North, the Council of Wales and the Marches, the Court of High Commission, the Court of the Duchy of Lancaster, and the Court of Exchequer of the County Palatine of Durham.

It is interesting to observe that the abolition of Star Chamber jurisdiction was placed in the forefront. This was because the mani-

festations of conciliar power in the Star Chamber, though selective
and occasional, were open for all to see, and Charles and his advisers,
notably during the ascendancy of Laud, had chosen offences against
the ecclesiastical hierarchy for public trial *in terrorem*. The offenders
had been treated with relentless severity. The cruel punishments
meted out to Leighton, Prynne, Burton, Bastwick and other libellers
of the bishops and of the Church Government had whipped up
general indignation both in the Houses and outside—particularly
in London, which was bitterly hostile to the hierarchy. London
mattered more than all the rest of the kingdom put together. A
large proportion of the members of the House of Commons were
either Puritans or at least sympathizers to a considerable extent with
the Puritan views on the powers of bishops. The old anti-clerical
feeling, always marked in England, was sharpened by the dominating
influence exercised by Archbishop Laud and his colleagues, and exacerbated by their 'Arminianism', though there was nothing new
about the Laudian severities, or about co-operation between the Star
Chamber and the ecclesiastical authorities.[1] But the times had
changed in 1641, and there is no doubt that the Star Chamber
suffered from the closeness of its connection with the extremely
unpopular High Commission. There was a long-standing sympathy
with ministers who had refused to conform, and this had been
intensified by the 'Arminian' (or Anglo-Catholic) complexion of
the Episcopal Bench. To the old-fashioned Anglican the abandonment of Calvinist (or Augustinian) theology appeared to be a
definite step towards reconciliation with Rome. The depth of the
feeling aroused can hardly be exaggerated.[2] It may well be that the
violence of the animosity which the 'Arminianism' of the bishops
inspired, together with the power of enforcing it which their
temporal authority gave them, assisted in persuading learned anti-

---

[1] In 1607 one Pemlie, a minister in Kent, was sentenced by the Council in the Star
Chamber (including the Archbishop of Canterbury, and the Bishop of London) for
libelling the episcopal government of the Church. He was sentenced to be fined
£2,000, to stand on the pillory at Westminster and there to lose one ear; to stand on
the pillory at Cheapside and there to lose the other ear; to be whipped at both places
unless he confessed his fault, and to be perpetually imprisoned, after having been
degraded from the ministry. The sentence was carried out. "First he had twenty-
five jerkes (lashes), and then stood in the pillory and had one of his eares cutte close
from his heade, and after that he had twenty-five jerkes more." *Les Reportes del
Cases in Camera Stellata, 1593-1609*, ed. W. P. Baildon, privately printed 1894,
p. 341.
[2] See *Life of Sir Simonds D'Ewes*, London 1845, Vol. II, p. 113.

quarian lawyers like D'Ewes to resuscitate the long discredited theory that Star Chamber jurisdiction originated in Henry VII's abortive act of 1487, as proof of its illegality and usurpations. But it does not seem possible to go further than this. The target of the opposition was the personal government of the King, not innovations in religion. The abolition of the Court of High Commission, and the stripping of ecclesiastical authority of every shred of temporal power, had robbed Episcopal Government of all its terrors.[1]

To begin with, a standing committee of the Commons was set up to consider 'the Reforming of the unlawful proceedings' in the Star Chamber. It was originally proposed to amend, not to abolish. Two bills were submitted to the Committee for consideration, but on May 31, 1641, Edmund Prideaux, a Common Lawyer, reported that it had decided that total abolition was necessary. There was some opposition, but this was stilled by Simonds D'Ewes, who played a prominent part in the debate. He said that the irregularities of the Court had been so great that no bill could effectively moderate them, and that therefore abolition was the only practical course. The House agreed without further demur. The "Act for the Regulating the Privy Council, and for taking away the Court commonly called the Star Chamber" was accordingly passed. It began by rehearsing the gist of 1.3 Henry VII, and went on to state that 'the said judges have not kept themselves to the points limited by the said statute, but have undertaken to punish where no law doth warrant.' Under cover of the blaze of anti-ecclesiastical fury in which the Star Chamber perished, the rest of conciliar jurisdiction, except that of the Court of Requests, was by the same Act swept away almost unnoticed.

The legal profession gained no advantage, indeed rather the reverse from the disappearance of the ancient Council in the Star Chamber, but it more than made up for this by the downfall of the other manifestations of conciliar judicial authority, especially that of the Councils of the North and of Wales and the Marches, and particularly of the Privy Council.

The hand of the Common Lawyer is clearly visible in the condemnation of the judicial activities of the Council Table. It is based entirely on the Council's efforts to save its many petitioners from

---

[1] For a different view see Last Years of the Star Chamber 1634–41, H. Phillips, Royal Historical Society's *Transactions*, 4th series, Vol. XXI, 1939.

being compelled to undergo the long delays and incur the often ruinous expense of 'the circuit of the law'.[1]

Conciliar government could if necessary have been carried on without the aid of the Star Chamber, the essential function of which was to give publicity to punishment when that was thought desirable. The abolition of the judicial authority of the Privy Council, which was the heart of the governmental machine, and of its power to commit to prison, was the fatal blow, not the abolition of 'the Court commonly called the Star Chamber', and it was effected, ostensibly at any rate, simply because of the Council's interference in civil cases and in the 'Course of the Courts'. The wealthier upper class, alone represented in Parliament, had as a whole no grievance against the Common Law, and the strong lawyer element were able to carry their allies with them in making the attempts of the executive to mitigate the oppressions of the legal system in favour of the shorn lamb the excuse not only for cancelling the ancient obligation of the King to do justice to all his subjects when for any reason they could not get it elsewhere, but also for destroying the old machinery of effective executive authority. In the future no action could be taken against anyone, however grasping, unsocial, or conscienceless his conduct might be, unless it were cognizable in the Courts of Common Law.

There is no doubt that the powers of the old conciliar government had often been abused, but their disappearance was soon widely lamented. Judge Hale, according to Sir Philip Warwick, was heard openly to say at an assize at Cambridge that he believed that since 'the pulling down of that Court (the Star Chamber) there had been in a few years more perjuries and frauds unpunished than there had been in a hundred years before'.[2] As is usually the case—even with Clarendon—he gave undue prominence to the Council in the Star Chamber, which attracted general attention owing to the publicity of its proceedings. The privy Council as such, without the aid of the Judges, or of Counsel, would have done most, if not all, of

[1] The charge against the Privy Council reads "The Council Table hath of late times assumed unto itself a power to intermeddle in civil causes and matters only of private interest between party and party, and have adventured to determine of the estates and liberties of the subject contrary to the law of the land, and the rights and privileges of the subject, by which great and manifold mischiefs and inconveniences have arisen and happened, and much uncertainty by means of such proceedings hath been conceived concerning men's rights and estates." Gardiner, *Constitutional Documents of the Puritan Revolution* 1625–60, pp. 181–2.

[2] Sir Philip Warwick, *Memoirs of the Reign of King Charles I*, London 1701, p. 175.

what was wanted. A consideration of its achievements in the social and economic fields, and its constant harrying of local magnates and officials during the 'Eleven Years' Tyranny' makes it permissible to conjecture that the horrors of what is known as the Industrial Revolution would have been considerably mitigated had the Central Government been able to maintain its executive authority unhampered by the Common Law.

No specific malfeasance was alleged in the Act against the Councils of the North and of Wales and the Marches. Both had become almost entirely civil Courts, and their involvement in the general downfall of conciliar institutions brought some grist to the lawyers' mill, and, on the negative side, removed from the local gentry the risk of being sued by their poorer neighbours and tenants.

Much as the Common Lawyers, and the upper classes generally, disliked the Court of Requests, it was not touched. The Long Parliament was not afraid of ill feeling in the North, now rendered fairly harmless, partly by disarmament, partly by the existence of a Scottish army friendly to themselves; or in Wales, where any formidable combination was unlikely. But they could not afford to risk discontent in London and the Home Counties, and the Court was undoubtedly popular. Its discontinuance by Act of Parliament would have been regarded as a reactionary measure and would have been widely resented. It was therefore never abolished, but as the Masters were all Royalists, it ceased to function when the Civil War broke out, save for formal sittings at Oxford, and was never revived as a judicial tribunal.

The unpopularity of the Civil Courts of Common Law among the less well-to-do classes was realized, and on occasion, when there was a need to conciliate them, reform was promised, though the promises were never fulfilled. The Grand Remonstrance of 1641, which was an appeal to the general public against the King and the House of Lords, contained a clause foreshadowing 'the regulating of Courts of Justice, and abridging both the delays and charges of lawsuits'.[1] The Long Parliament was getting nervous, and was seeking to placate all those interested in the struggle with the King's Government by holding out hopes of better things, when the bishops and Popish lords in the Upper House ceased to be able to thwart their endeavours. But while the power of the Long Parliament continued and the

[1] *Constitutional Documents of the Puritan Revolution*, ed. Gardiner, 3rd ed., p. 224, article 140.

Civil War diverted attention from the ordinary business of life, the lawyers were in no danger of losing the advantages they had gained. Not till the defeat of the victorious Parliament by its own army, and the rise of Cromwell to political power, was the Common Law in danger, in even greater danger, perhaps, than it had been during the ascendancy of Wolsey.

In conclusion, before the end of 1641 the basis on which the 'new monarchy' had rested had been gravely weakened. The King could still choose his own Councillors, and was still the head of the executive, but his absolute dependence on Parliament for supply was bound to result in his having to dismiss unpopular ministers, and to abandon unpopular policies. The ancient obligations of the kingship to protect the people from foreign or domestic danger, and to do justice to all men, had been so undermined and restricted as to be untranslatable into action by the King alone.

The country had outgrown its ancient 'constitution', which had come to result in an inescapable series of deadlocks. Their continued recurrence had been made impossible by the defeat of the King's Government. The indefeasible prerogative of the King to govern absolutely could never again be asserted in practice. The indefeasible prerogative of the subject—his right to his property and his status as a free man—was still maintained, though its ultimate disappearance was already foreshadowed by the birth of the doctrine of the sovereignty of Parliament.

CHAPTER XIX

CONCLUSION

IT is desirable to consider briefly the part played by the grievance against the administration of justice in bringing about the upheaval of 1642, and the troubles of the Interregnum.

To what extent the long-drawn troubles in Ireland which culminated in the rebellion of 1641 were due to hatred of the English legal system it is impossible to say, but it seems that there is some truth in John Cook's vigorously expressed view. He described in graphic terms the 'cannibalization' of the unfortunate Irish, driven from one Court—and country—to another in the vain search for justice. As long before as 1227 a collection of writs had been sent to Ireland for the use of the newly established Irish Chancery, and the new scheme of 'common law' justice was applied to the native Irish of the Pale in all its rigour, but by the later Middle Ages a great part of the country had relapsed to Irish law and custom. The Tudors had endeavoured to bring this state of things to an end, with unhappy results, partly owing to the fact that their administration of Ireland, judicial, executive, and financial, was rotten to the core. Bacon protested against the retention of the English judicial system, at any rate until the country had recovered from the desolation of the Elizabethan reconquest, and recommended the introduction of summary and presumably equitable justice.[1] But his advice was not taken, and in 1607 the extension of the English system into their territories caused the great chieftain O'Neill of Tyrone, and also O'Donnell and Maguire to flee to Spain. In November 1640 the Committee for Irish affairs reported that many petitions of suitors from the Courts in Ireland were pending, and that the petitioners in many cases had come to an end of their resources.[2] It is perhaps therefore justifiable to ascribe the introduction of English Common Law and English Equity some share in the causes of the rising of

---

[1] Bacon, *Considerations touching the Queen's Service in Ireland,* Works, ed. B. Montagu, Vol. V.

[2] John Rushworth, *Historical Collections,* ed. of 1721, Vol. IV, p. 65.

1641, which directly resulted in the Houses of Parliament grasping at the power of the sword, and passing the Militia Ordinance which was the signal for the outbreak of the Civil War.

The triumph of the Common Lawyers in 1641 depended for its permanence on the continued supremacy of the Parliament and the classes represented therein. The defeat of the Parliament by 'that rebel rout, its first upholders', at once endangered the whole time-honoured legal system.[1]

The great historians of the period, Gardiner and Firth, paid remarkably little attention to the bitter struggle for law reform and the light it threw upon the fate of both the King and the two Houses —a struggle which began as soon as the war was won and was intensified when the lower middle class gained admission to the seats of power, and with which Cromwell himself came to sympathize. But there seems to be little doubt that next to liberty of conscience for 'the godly', the complete remodelling of the structure of the law and of the procedure and practice of the Courts in order to secure a fair deal for the small man was what lay nearest to the hearts of the class on whose good will both the Commonwealth and the Protectorate largely depended.

For some time after the defeat of the King, the monarchy was blamed for the failures of justice. Charles was the heir of William the Norman, and the Common Law was regarded as an importation by the Conqueror, and the cherished engine of the still surviving 'Norman tyranny'. Signs of 'Anti-Normanism' had been noticeable for centuries. Towards the close of Edward I's reign the author of the "Mirror of Justices"—perhaps Andrew Horn, a London fish-monger—had expressed with a wealth of highly imaginative instances, the superiority of the ancient laws and usages of England, as administered by Alfred. Among the abuses he enumerates was the failure to fix the fees of pleaders.[2]

Allusion has already been made to Starkey's outspoken condemnation of the Common Law and its antique Norman garb in the dialogue between Pole and Lupset. In the reign of Elizabeth, Lord Brooke wrote that the Common Law made 'Judges, and not princes great',[3] and gave the lawyers an opportunity to raise them-

---

[1] Contemporary Ballad, quoted by C. H. Firth in Ballad History of Charles I, Royal Historical Society's *Transactions*, 3rd series, Vol. VI, 1912.

[2] *The Mirror of Justices*, ed. W. J. Whittaker, Selden Society, 1895, pp. 159 and 166–71.

[3] Lord Brooke, *Treatise of Monarchy*, Works, ed. Grosart, Vol. I, § VII.

selves above both truth and thrones. He recognized that the protraction of processes and trials cried for reform, and the use of a
generally unknown dialect raised in his mind the question whether
it would not be better to have no law at all. The Histories of
England published in the late sixteenth and early seventeenth
centuries, and widely read, expressed bitter hostility to the English
legal system, which was traced to the Conquest, and regarded as a
badge of national slavery. It was probably from these works, by
Holinshed, Speed, Daniel and Martyn, especially Daniel, that the
Levellers and others drew their view as to the origin of their miseries.
Daniel admitted that there might be some ancient English survivals
in the Common Law, but recognized that most of the substance and
practice of it was Norman in origin, and attributed its technicality
and complications to the contentious and litigious spirit of the
Normans, which was alien to the alleged simplicity and straight-
forwardness of the Anglo-Saxons. The law was the one surviving
mark of the subjection of the English, 'and that still speaks French to
us in England'.[1] William Martyn (Historie and lives of the Kings of
England, 1638) says that William 'tired out the English nation with
extraordinary troubles and excessive charges in the prosecution of
their suits in law'.

After the defeat of the King, anti-Normanism found more general
and violent expression. Pease, writing of the Leveller movement,
says of its leaders and agents "they saw behind them a Norman
Conquest not passed away six centuries before, but a Norman
Conquest out of which they had climbed in the past few years,
setting their feet at Marston Moor and Naseby." Until the clergy
ceased to be sustained by tithes, the institution of which was also
attributed to the Conqueror (to ensure that the priests 'preached him
up') and the tediousness, ambiguities and uncertainties of the legal
system had been swept away, England was still under the iron
Norman Yoke. The writings of the Leveller propagandists, especially
Lilburne, Overton, Walwyn and Wildman abound in condem-
nations of the practice of the Courts, in demands for instant and
radical reform, and in abusive references to professional lawyers 'the
Vermin, plagues, and pests of a commonwealth'. As early as July
1646 Overton wrote "Ye know, the laws of this nation are unworthy
a free people, and deserve from first to last to be considered, and

[1] Samuel Daniel, *The Collection of the History of England 1615*, fifth edition, 1685,
p. 43.

seriously debated, and reduced to an agreement with common equity and right reason. . . Magna Carta itself being but a beggarly thing, containing many marks of intolerable bondage. The Norman way for ending of controversies was much more abusive than the English way, yet the Conqueror contrary to his oath, introduced the Norman laws, and his litigious and vexatious way amongst us. He erected a trade of judges and lawyers, to sell justice and injustice at his own unconscionable rate and in what time he pleased; the corruption whereof is yet remaining upon us, to our continual impoverishing and molestation, from which we thought you should have delivered us."[1] In 1648 John Lilburne stated "it is a Badge of our Slavery to a Norman Conqueror to have our laws in the French tongue, and it is little less than brutish vasselage to be bound to walk by laws which the people cannot know."[2] He went on to demand that 'our native right be restored to us, which is now also the price of our blood.' In 1649 one John Warr wrote in a pamphlet entitled "The corrupt interest of lawyers in this Commonwealth" that "the laws of England are full of Tricks, Doubts, and contrary to themselves; for they were invented and contrived by the Normans, which were of all nations the most quarrelsome, and most fallacious in contriving of Controversies and Suits."[3] The lawyers, according to Winstanley, the Digger leader, were deliberately created agents of oppression, keeping the law in French and Latin to make it unintelligible to the vulgar, and thus being able to serve the turn of the landowning gentry who alone could afford to pay their fees. "England", he wrote, "is a prison, the varieties of subtleties in the laws preserved by the sword are the bolts, bars, and doors of the prison; the lawyers are the gaolers, and poor men are the prisoners." (A New Year's Gift). The centralization of the Courts at Westminster was also a constantly ventilated grievance. Lilburn's ideal was the wholly imaginary Anglo-Saxon golden age when, he believed, all suits were promptly and equitably decided on the spot by juries of neighbours, without trouble or expense.

Suspicions began to dawn early (they are traceable in the 'Remon-

---

[1] Richard Overton, Remonstrance of Many Thousand Citizens, printed in *Leveller Manifestoes*, ed. D. M. Wolfe, Thomas Nelson & Sons, 1944.

[2] A Declaration of some Proceedings of Lt. Colonel John Lilburne, Articles 5 and 6 of "The Earnest Petition of Many Freeborn people of this Nation" addressed to "the Supream Authority of England, the Commons assembled in Parliament", published February 1648.

[3] *Harleian Miscellany*, ed. of 1808 et seq., Vol. III.

strance of many Thousand Citizens' of July 1646) that the Parliament was not at all anxious for the reform of the law, or for the abolition of privilege, and that those who stood to gain by the victory in the Civil War were not those who had ridden in the ranks.[1]

What the lower middle class people, who constituted the bulk of the Leveller party and its sympathizers, wanted was individual liberty, both liberty of conscience and also freedom to do the best they could for themselves in the affairs of this world. Unless the law were radically altered, a fair share of opportunity would continue to be denied to them. They got practically nothing out of the Commonwealth, and it was not long before they began to realize that they had fought on the wrong side; that the 'Norman tyrant' had done what he could for them in the face of great odds; and that in spite of the maintenance of ancient privileges and the grant of new ones, especially monopolies, and even in spite of the imposition of Laudian uniformity, the government they had got was worse than than the one they had overthrown. Though it was chiefly the religious problem which caused swords to be drawn, the desire for law reform was at least a strong contributory cause of the rebellion against the King, and was a powerful factor in securing support for the heirs of the old feudal class, which might otherwise not have been forthcoming. John Cook, the regicide, would have gone further. "I am sure", he wrote "it was Corruptions and Oppressions in Courts of Justice, that made England first sick, and the end of that must either be the Disburthening of Nature, or the Dissolving of Nature, the former whereof I wait and Pray for. . . . This one great thing [reform of the legal system] that my Honoured friends in the Army told me they Fought for, and myself as being formerly a member thereof, Ingaged with them, and I feare the least breach of an Ingagement more than all the Uncircumcized Philistines. Covetous Chirurgeons that keep the Wound rawe and Torment the Patient to

[1] The failure to achieve this after the King's defeat caused much bitter comment. In the 'Case of the Armie truly stated' possibly written by Wildman, and published in 1647, it is stated that "a Committee of conscientious persons be forthwith selected to consider of the most intollerable oppressions by unjust proceedings in law, that withal the lawes might be reduced to a smaller number to be comprised in one volume in the English tongue, that every free Commoner might understand his own proceedings, that Courts might be in the respective counties or hundreds, that proceedings might become short & speedy, & that the numberless grievances in the law & lawyers might be redressed as soone as possible." Lilburne complained in his 'England's New Chains Discovered', "There is not one perplexity or absurdity in proceedings taken away." See *Leveller Tracts*, Haller and Davies, p. 162.

gett more money for the cure, Lett such be excoriated. I should
think myself a Violator and Betrayer of the Honour and Justice of
the Army, if I should not promote such an Expedient with my
petitionary Earnestnesse." In another passage he alluded to the
longing for freedom from "the Norman Yoake", as exemplified in
the "Old Courts and tedious formalities, which good men hoped
would have an Honourable Interrment and Burial in the Sepulchre
of Monarchy". He closed his denunciation by saying "The summe
of all is this—I have been for many Yeares convinced of the Horrible
Injuries and Oppressions that the Poor People of England and
Ireland have suffered and Groaned under by this Grand Cheat and
Abominable Idoll call'd the Course of the Courts. I have prayed
earnestly to Allmighty God for a Reformation. I have drawn and
Signed many Petitions to that effect. It hath been the longing Desire
of the Good People of England to have it effected, but it was Lookt
upon as a Worke insuperable, and the Sonns of Zeruiah were too
hard for the faithfull Patriotts of the Nations."[1]

Hope had begun to dawn when the 'Barebones' Parliament, in
which the lower middle class had a strong majority, launched its
vigorous programme of law reform. It began by abolishing
Chancery, the delays and expense of which had caused it to surpass
the Common Law Courts in unpopularity, but had not time to set
up machinery to take its place. The fears of the conservative leaders
were soon aroused by the attack on tithes, largely in the ownership
of lay impropriators, which seemed to presage an assault on other
forms of property, perhaps even rents, and the dissolution of the
Parliament of Saints speedily followed.

Nothing was definitely or permanently achieved under the
Protectorate, in spite of the growing sympathy of Cromwell. It
seems that he came to realize the pressing need for law reform as a
result of reading a letter from John Cook, which seems to have been
similar in content to that to the Lord Deputy of Ireland, which has
already several times been quoted. Until long after his rise to power
he appears to have realized the bitterness of discontent induced by
the working of the legal system only dimly. Unlike most of the
country gentlemen of his day, he had, as he said himself, as little
knowledge of the law as he had of arithmetic, and had clearly never
been entered in an Inn of Court. What lay nearest his heart, indeed

[1] John Cook to the Lord Deputy of Ireland. Printed in *Ireland in the Seventeenth
Century*, McLysaght.

almost to the exclusion of all else, was the desire to achieve liberty of conscience. But he was deeply impressed by Cook's letter, which he discussed with Ludlow. In his account of this conversation, Ludlow says "It was his intention to make a thorow reformation of the clergy and Law; but said he" [in the words of Cook] "The sons of Zeruiah are yet too strong for us, and we cannot mention the reformation of the law, but they presently cry out we design to destroy propriety; whereas the law, as it is now constituted, serves only to maintain the lawyers, and to encourage the rich to oppress the poor; affirming that Mr. Cook then Justice in Ireland, by proceeding in a summary and expeditious way, determined more causes in a week than Westminster Hall in a year; saying further that Ireland was a clean paper in that particular, and capable of being governed by such laws as shall be found most agreeable to justice; which may be so impartially administered, as to be a good precedent even to England itself; where when they once perceive propriety preserved at an easy and cheap rate in Ireland, they will never permit themselves to be so cheated and abused as now they are."[1]

Cook's letter undoubtedly brought home to Cromwell the necessity of tackling the thorny problem of law reform as soon as possible. At the opening of Parliament on September 17, 1656 he said "There is one general Grievance in the Nation. It is the Law."[2] In his speech of April 21, 1657 he said "I hope you will think sincerely, as before God, that the laws must be regulated; I hope you will. We have been often talking of them, and I remember well, in the old Parliament, that we were more than three months and could not get over the word 'encumbrance'. And then we thought that there was little hope of regulating the law, when there was such a difficulty as that. But surely the laws need to be regulated! And I must needs say I think it is a sacrifice acceptable to God on many accounts, and I am persuaded it is one thing that God looks for and would have. I confess, if any man would ask me 'why, how would you have it done?' I confess I do not know how. But I think verily at the least, the delays in suits, and those various things that I do not know what names they bear—I have heared talk of 'demurrers' and such like things as I scarce know—but I say certainly that the people are greatly suffering in this respect; they are so."[3]

---

[1] *Edmund Ludlow, Memoirs*, ed. C. H. Firth, Oxford 1894, Vol. I, pp. 246–7.
[2] *Letters and Speeches of Oliver Cromwell*, ed. Carlyle, Part IX, Speech V, p. 185.
[3] *Letters and Speeches of Oliver Cromwell*, ed. Carlyle, Part X, p. 288.

But Cromwell, like Wolsey, was too much occupied with other pressing problems at home and abroad to give the time and thought necessary for the systematic tackling of an ancient and deeply rooted system. Also skilled professional assistance was not forthcoming. So long established and powerful a vested interest could be destroyed only by a revolution. The Revolution had indeed come, but it had been the work of the politically minded upper class, and the Common Lawyers, the most solidly entrenched of all Conservatives, had taken a leading part in it, and had indeed been the spearhead of the attack on the old order. In the end, after a brief period of apprehension owing to the influence suddenly acquired by the lower middle class element in the army and outside it, only those parts of the old order perished which were displeasing to the upper classes.

The Restoration was a Restoration of Parliament as much as of the King. Its architects, chief of whom was Hyde, a Common Lawyer and an antediluvian conservative, were passionately anti-militarist, and fully aware of the dangers of a standing army. The King was the King of 1641, stripped of the powers which the prerogative Courts had given him, and the Parliament was also that of 1641, of the same social complexion and prejudices, but strengthened by the claim to participate in executive government which the experiences of the Interregnum had given it. The real victors of the Civil Wars were the lawyers, who were enabled to retain intact the fruits of their triumph over the King's Government.

INDEX

INDEX

Account, 25, 37–8, 39
Accusations, false, 36, 109, 111
Adams, G. B., 29
Administration of assets, 38
Admiralty, Court of, 23 n. 3, 53, 123–4
Advocates, 19, 20, 26, 32, 49, 78, 93, 94, 107, 128, 133, 152
Anglo-Saxon elements in English law, 9–10, 163
Appeal of felony, 45
Aristotle, 15, 93–4
Arminianism, 156
Army, disillusionment of the, after the Cival War, 164–6
Arrest, of a defendant, 20–1; powers of, 46
Assumpsit, 38, 41
Attaint, jury and writ of, 44
Attorney-General, 105, 107
Attorneys, 19, 32, 83–5, 96, 111, 121, 126

Bacon, Francis, 56, 60, 111, 112, 122, 123, 132, 133, 141–2, 161
Baildon, W. P., 61, 107
Baldwin, J. F., 58, 61, 63
Bancroft, Archbishop, 130
Barbour, W. T., 2
Bartholomew de Cotton, 55
Bates' case, 135
Battle, trial by, 11, 43
Benefit of clergy, 46–7
Bentham, 95
Bereford (C. J.), 25–6
Berkeley, Judge, 153
Blackstone, 42, 81, 92
Bolland, W. C., 27
Bracton, 17, 25
Brinklow, Henry, 20 n. 2

Brooke, Lord, 28, 86 n. 1, 162–3
Bryce, James, 150 n. 1
Buckingham, George Villiers, 1st Duke of, 141, 142, 145, 149
Burton, Robert, 77, 85 n. 3
Bushell's case, 30 n. 1

Cade, Jack, 38 n. 1, 41 n. 1, 53
Caesar, Sir Julius, 125
Canon Law, 16, 19, 25, 29, 31, 35, 53, 70, 78, 93
Carey's *Present State of England*, 84 n. 1
Cavendish, George, 70, 71 n. 1
Cawdrey's case, 129
Censorship of books, 104
Centralization of justice, 11-12, 26–8, 32–3, 164, 165 n. 1
'Certainty', 30, 46, 92
Chambers, Richard, 153
Champerty, 36, 52
Chancellor, Lord, 58, 80, 81, 104, 105; position of, 35, 91–2; common lawyers replace ecclesiastics as, 77–8, 94–5, 107 *see also* Chancery
Chancery, as source of royal writs, 10–11, 12, 13, 25, 26, 35; Court of, separated from Council, 34–5; equitable jurisdiction of, 30, 34–42, 51, 61, 66, 74, 77, 92–4, 124; in 16th and 17th centuries 70–1, 78, 80, 81–4, 91–7, 113–14; procedure of, 39–40, deterioration in, 92–7; Common Law Courts, their struggle with, 118–22, their defeat by, 122, influence upon them of, 122–3; abolition of, decreed by Barebones Parliament, 166
Charles I, King, 88, 89, 90, 95 n. 3, 100, 124, 126, 131, 136, 142, 144–62

Civil Law, civilians, see Roman Law

Clapham, John, 86

Clarendon, see Hyde, Edward

Classes, poorer, 6, 7, 27, 75, 122, 165–6; upper, 3, 4–7, 28, 48–51, 75, 76, 77, 89, 117, 131, 158–9, 168 see also Lawyers, Levellers, 'Overmighty' subjects, Requests, Trade

Clerkships, 32, 81–4, 95, 96, 111–12, 119, 126

Coinage, 101, 104, 137

Coke, Sir Edward, 14, 20, 60, 110, 119, 121–2, 123–131, 135, 137, 138–9, 140–4 passim, 146–7, 152, 154

'Colour', 22, 37

Common Bench, see Common Pleas

Common Law, feudal element in, 2–3, 8, 10; and jury trial, 43–4; property, essentially a law of, 6, 9, 13–14, 43 n. 1, 136; public law, as foundation of, 2–3, 6, 142, 155, 160; radical reform of, failure to achieve, 7, 8, 35, 41, 56, 72–8, 94, 132, 159, 162–7

Common Pleas, Court of, 20, 25, 26, 29, 55, 73, 79, 80, 82, 83, 85, 106, 119, 124, 154

Compurgation, 10, 11, 39

Conspiracy, 36–7, 109

Contract, 14, 22, 37, 38–9, 41, 119, 122

Coronation oath, 9, 51, 63, 136

Cook, John, 8, 82 n. 3, 96, 113, 120–1, 161, 165–7

Cooke, William, 95–6

Council, see King's Council and Privy Council

Council of the North, 53–4, 65, 69, 70, 98, 126, 127–8, 157

Council of Wales, 53–4, 65–6, 69–70, 126–8, 159

'Course of the Courts', 3, 6, 39, 75, 113, 158, 166

Covenant, 38

Cowell, John, 142

Cranfield, Lionel, 1st Earl of Middlesex, 88, 141, 142

Crew (C. J.), 145, 152

Croke, Judge, 148, 150, 151

Cromwell, Oliver, 23, 154, 162, 166–8

Cromwell, Thomas, 73, 75, 99

Crown, and the Common Law, 7, 10–11, 28–9, 56, 73; as fountain of justice, 9, 10–11, 26, 29, 34, 93; limits to power of, 2 n.2, 3, 4–6; revenues of, 3–4, 7, 12, 48, 55–6, 73–4, 79, 134, 139; the subject and, 3, 4, 5–6, 130–1, 160 see also Chapters XVII, XVIII passim, Coronation Oath, King's Council, New Monarchy, Proclamations.

Curia Regis, 6, 10, 11, 12

Daniel, Samuel, 163

Darcy v. Allin, 140

Davison, Secretary, 100

Debt, 39, 115–17

Dedimus potestatem, writ of, 40

Defamation, 102, 109

Detinue, 39

D'Ewes, Sir Simonds, 14, 81, 133, 157

Dialogus de Scaccario, 17

Dicey, A. V., 35, 61

Dickens, Charles, 31, 96 n. 5

Distraint, writs of, 20–1

Dudley, Edmund, 56, 57, 58

Duplicity (pleading), 23

Dyer's Reports, 78

Ecclesiastical courts, 109, 129–30

Edward, King, I, 7, 13, 17, 19, 28–9, 55; II, 43; III, 7, 34, 49, 52, 56, 98, 140; IV, 3, 34, 36, 50, 52, 60, 128, 140; VI, 48, 61, 98, 118

Egerton, Lord Keeper, 83 n. 2

Ejectment, 122

Eldon, Lord Chancellor, 92

'Eleven Years' Tyranny', the, 149, 153, 159

Eliot, Sir John, 152

Elizabeth I, Queen, 59, 88, 94, 99, 108, 112, 113, 123, 126, 131, 138, 139–41

Embracery, 52, 59

Empson, Richard, 56, 57, 58, 64

Enclosures, 101

English, statute ordering pleadings in, 18

Equity, 9, 25–6, 118–19, 120–1, 122;
disappearance of, from Common Law
courts, 25–33, from Chancery, 92–4
See also Chancellor *and* Chancery
Erasmus, 20
Error, writ of, 24
Essoins, 21
Exchequer, Court of, 29, 79, 106, 135,
152
Eyre, 26–8, 33, 34

Fact, issues of, 11, 22–3, 37, 43, 53, 144–
5, 150–1
Fawkes, Guy, 102 n. 3
Fealty, 2, 3
Felony, 51
Finch, Lord Keeper, 154
Five Knights, case of the, 145–7, 150
Fleet prison, 116
Fleta, 100
Forced Loan, 145–7
Forgery, 108–9, 111
Fortescue, Sir John, 3, 20, 43–4, 49, 79
Franchises, 39–40, 46, 51
Fraud, 108–9, 158
Freehold, 2, 6, 9, 10, 11, 12, 26–7, 43,
44, 51, 74, 137, 138; offices held as,
80, 82, 86, 95, 116
French, Norman, use of, 16, 18–19, 26,
132, 163, 164

Gaol Delivery, commissions of, 27, 45
Gerson, John, 93
Giustinian, S., 70
Glanville's case, 121–2
Goodman, Bishop, 85–6
Grand Remonstrance, 159
Gray's Inn, 151–2

Habeas corpus, 145–6
Hakewill, 135–6, 141, 142, 150
Hale (C. J.), 46, 82, 84, 85, 158
Hall, Edward, 68, 69
Hallam, 62
Hampden's case, 149–151, 153, 154

Harrison, W., 32 n. 1
Haslewood, W., 96 n. 5
Hatton, Sir Christopher (L. C.), 94, 107,
114
Hayes' *Dialogue*, 22 n. 1
Hengham, R. de, (C. J.), 55
Henry, King, I, 10, 11; II, 11–12, 43, 55;
III, 10, 12–13; IV, 130; VI, 36, 49, 106;
VII, 46, 52, 55–66, 69, 98, 106, 111;
VIII, 46, 58, 61, 62 n. 1, 67, 68, 73–8,
79, 88, 89, 94, 97, 98–9, 111, 118, 130
'Heraldry', 96
Hereditaments, 14
High Commission, 129–30, 156–7
Hoby, Sir Philip, 98
Holdsworth, Sir William, 19, 21, 34–5,
48, 55–6, 80, 82, 95
Household, King's, 60–1, 68, 99
Hudson, W., 83 n. 2, 109–12,
Hundred Court, 10, 11, 12, 34
Hyde, (C. J.), 146
Hyde, Edward, 1st Earl of Clarendon,
93 n. 3, 151, 158, 162

Impeachment, 141–2, 154
Impositions, 134–7, 153
Indictments, 45–7
Inns of Court, 8, 16, 19–20, 30–1, 49, 78,
129, 151–2
Interregnum, 164–8
Ireland, 120, 161–2, 167
Italian Relation of England, 47
Itinerant Justices, 26–8, 33, 34

James I, King, 88, 90, 94, 95, 113, 121–2,
127, 131–3, 134–43
Jeofail, statutes of, 24, 45
Judges, 7–8, 19, 20, 25–9 *passim*, 45, 55,
71–8, 106–7, 142–3, 145, 152–4
Judges' Judgment, The, 153–4
Judicature Acts of 1873, 122
Jury, 7, 10, 11, 22, 36, 43–4, 51, 53, 58,
59, 61, 101, 110, 111
Justices of the Peace, 45, 46, 101

Kern, F., 2 n. 2

King, *see* Crown

King's Bench, Court of, 18, 29, 55, 79, 80, 82, 83, 85, 106, 111, 119, 142, 153

King's Council, 13, 18, 29, 57, 64, 68–9, 91, 98–100, 129, 137–9; cases referred to Chancery, 34–5, 51; civil law business under Elizabeth and James I, 113–17; committees of, 57–8, 63, 69, 88, 89, 98; criminal jurisdiction from 1540, 99–112; judicial powers, ancient exercise of, by, 34, 51, 52–3, 59, 63, 65, 123, statutory limits to, 51, abolished, 157–9; meetings in Star Chamber held usually (till 1540) for executive or judicial purposes, 37, 52, 58, 60, 61, 67–9, 98–9; public order, concern of, with, 50–2, 58, 65, 102 *See also* Curia Regis, King's Council in the Star Chamber, King's Council learned in the Law, Privy Council, Star Chamber

King's Council in the Star Chamber, i.e., from 1540, for criminal trials by the Privy Council assisted by the Judges, 59, 78, 83 n. 2, 84, 91, 99–112, 128–9, 138; distinguished by publicity from trials at the Council Table, 99, 102–5; procedure of, 105–6, 107, 110–12; abolition of, 155–8 *see also* Star Chamber

King's Council Learned in the Law, 57–8, 65

Land Law, 12–14, 16, 17–18, 22, 26, 38, 39, 58, 80, 122; settlements, 76–7

Langland, William, 31

Latin, use of, 18, 19, 164

Laud, Archbishop, 95 n. 3, 149, 151, 156

Law, English attitude to, 1–3; fundamental, 6, 144, 152, 154; of God, 2–3, 71; of Nature, 71; and order 48; study of, *see* Inns of Court, Universities. *See also* Canon Law, Common Law, Equity, Land Law, Roman Law

Law Merchant, 122–4

Law terms, 32, 38, 90, 99, 107

Lawyers, allied with upper classes, 5, 49–50, 75, 80; Common, monopoly of legal business by, 19, 78; income of, 76, 79–86, 95–6, 119, 128, 162; profession of lay, 19–20; unpopularity of, 8, 31, 38 n. 1, 73, 86, 96 n. 5, 112, 163–4 *see also* Advocates, Attorneys, Clerkships, Inns of Court, Judges, Sergeants at Law, Solicitors

Leadam, I. S., 61, 89

L'Estrange, Sir Roger 4–5

Levellers, 154–5, 163–5

Libel, 109

Lilburne, John, 163–4, 165 n. 1

Littleton's *Tenures*, 14

Livery, *see* Maintenance

Locke, John, 5

Long Parliament, 151–160, 161, 162

Magna Carta, 108, 140, 144, 145–7, 152, 164

Maintenance, livery and, 36, 50, 52, 59, 61, 65, 108, 110

Maitland, F. W., 1, 10, 11, 13, 19, 28, 29, 31, 43, 76, 77, 78

Manchester, Edward Montagu, 1st Earl of, 90

Manning's case, 109

Mansfield, Chief Baron, 7

Martyn, William, 163

Mary I, Queen, 57, 61, 94, 99, 107, 138

Mercantile law, 122–4

Mesne process, 20–1

Militia Ordinance, 154, 162

Mirror of Justices, 162

Mompesson, Sir Giles, 141

Monasteries, dissolution of, 5, 77, 80

Monopolies, 131, 139–141

More, Sir Thomas, 6 n. 1, 73, 91–2

Newgate prison, 103

'New Monarchy', 1, 41, 141, 160

Norburie, George, 92 n. 3, 95, 96

Norman Conquest, blamed for Common Law defects, 162–6

North, Lord Keeper, 81, 96; Roger, 81, 91

Novel Disseisin, 11, 27

Noy, William, 141, 153

Ordeals, 9, 11, 43
Ore tenus, 166, 106
Outlawry to compel attendance, 21
'Overmighty' subjects, 36–7, 44, 48–52, 65, 68, 104, 108, 128
Overton, Richard, 163–4
Owen of Henlyn, George, 127
Oxford, Provisions of, 13; University of, 19, 78
Oyer et terminer, commission of, 52

Palgrave, Sir Francis, 50
Parker, Henry, 154, 155
Parliament, resists encroachments on Common Law, 41, 49–50, 51–2, 63–4, 77–8; lawyers in, 49, 76, 77, 151; supports Henry VII, 65; under the Stuarts, 134–162 *passim*
Partnership, 38
Paston Letters, 48
Paulet, Sir William, 103–4
Peachie's case, 140
Pecock, Bishop, 60
Pemlie's case, 156 n. 1
Pepys, 149
Perjury, 100–101, 108–9, 158
Petition of Right (1621), 146–7
Pickthorn, K. W. M., 61
Pilgrimage of Grace, 77, 127
Piracy, 101, 116, 149
Plowden, Edmund, 59, 62
Plucknett, T. F. T. 6 n. 2, 43, 77
Pollard, A. F., 8, 60–1, 98, 100
Pollock, Sir Frederick, 1, 8, 17–18
Pone, writ of, 11
Poor men's causes, *see* Requests, Court of and Requests jurisdiction
Popham (C. J.), 137
Praecipe, writ of, 12
Praemunire, statute of, 121
Press censorship, 104
Privy Council, 57, 98–9; after 1540 identical with King's Council, *q.v.*
Privy Seal, Keeper of, 58, 63, 90, 105
Proclamations, royal, 62 n. 1, 101, 102, 108, 137–9, 155
Puritans, 101, 129–30, 131, 134

Pym, John, 151, 152

Rashdall, Hastings, 16
Recordari, writ of, 11
Recusants, 100, 101
Reformation, 78, 131
Replication of a Sergeante, 30, 76, 93 n. 1, 118–19
Requests, Court of, 52, 63–5, 69, 80, 88–90, 113, 114, 115; Master of, in Star Chamber, 106; attacks on, 124–6; end of, 159
Requests jurisdiction, of King's Council, 69, 113–14, 125; of Councils of the North and of Wales, 65, 66, 69–70, 125–7; of Justices, 69, 125
Restoration, the, 168
Richard, King, II, 34, 41, 50, 93; III, 36 n. 3, 52, 63–4, 127
Richard of Ely, 17
Riots, 53, 58, 59, 61, 65, 68, 101
Robinson, R., 83 n. 1, n. 2
Rolls, Master of the, 64, 71, 92, 118
Roman Law, 3, 16, 19, 25–6, 29, 31, 44, 53, 64, 75, 78, 88, 89, 95 n. 3, 118, 119, 123
Roses, Wars of the, 50, 52, 65

St. Germain, Christopher, 71, 93, 119
St. John, Oliver, 149
Salisbury, Robert Cecil, 1st Earl of, 134, 135
Sanctuary, 46–7
Scholasticism, 15–16, 30–2, 93–4
Scofield, Cora L., 106
Scots Law, equity in, 31
Sealed instruments, 38–9
Seignorial courts, 10, 11, 12, 34
Selden, 30 n. 2, 40, 94, 146
Seneca, 4
Sergeants at law, 20, 79–80, 83 n. 2
Sheriff, 12, 20, 44, 49, 58, 59, 61
Ship money, 136, 141, 147–151, 153, 154
Shire Courts, 10, 11, 12, 28, 34
Skelton, John, 66, 67–8, 71 n. 2

Slander, 109

Smith, Sir Thomas, 32 n. 1, 59, 105

Solicitors, 83 n. 2, 96, 111

Somerset, Protector, 88–9, 118

Southampton, Earl of, (L. C.), 118

Specialty, 39

Star Chamber, Act of 1487, abortive committee of Council created by, 58–9, 62, opinions of the Act's effect, 58–62, 106–7, 157; 'Court' of, 59, 104, abolished, 62 see also King's Council in the Star Chamber, and King's Council, meetings in Star Chamber

Starkey, Thomas, 75, 162

Statutes, 10, 32, 60, 137–8

Stenton, F. M., 10

Stillington (L. C.), 40

Strafford, see Wentworth

Supremacy, Royal, over the Church, 131, 134; Act of (1559), 129–30

Tanner, J. R., 90 n. 1, 103–4, 143

Thorpe, (C. J.), 7

Tithes, 129–30, 163, 166

Tonnage and Poundage, 153

Torture, 102

Trade, growth of, 13, 37, 39, 116, 134; regulation of, 139 see also Law Merchant

Trailbaston, commissions of, 27

Treason, 51, 62 n. 1

Trespass, 13 n. 1, 28, 38, 41, 122

Trusts, 37, 122

Twysden, Sir Roger, 5

Universities, 15–16, 19, 30, 78

Uses, 37, 74–7

Vaughan, (C. J.), 30 n. 1

Venire facias, writ of, 111

Vergil, Polydore, 71 n. 1

Walter, Chief Baron, 152

Wantage Code, 10

Warr, John, 164

Warwick, Sir Philip, 158

Wentworth, Thomas, later Earl of Strafford, 126, 149

Westminster II, Statute of, 13, 34

White Hall, Court of Requests (q.v.) in the, 69, 125

Whitelocke, James, 107–8, 135, 136–7

Whitgift, Archbishop, 129

Wildman, Sir John, 163, 165 n. 1

Williams, Bishop (L. C.), 94, 107, 133

Wills, devising of land by, 74–7; Statute of, 77

Wilson, Thomas, 5, 78, 80, 86 n. 1

Winfield, P. H., 36, 39

Wingfield, Sir Robert, 98

Winstanley, Gerard, 164

Witchcraft, 43

Wolsey, Thomas, Cardinal, 7, 52, 58, 59, 67–72, 88, 91–2, 98–9, 104

Writs, 2, 9, 10–13, 16, 17, 18, 20–1, 24, 25, 26–8, 32, 34–8 passim, 40, 44, 111, 120, 145–6; in consimili casu, 13; judicial, 20, 80, 83; of privy seal, 53, 61, 64

Written word, authority of the, 15, 17, 23

Year Books, 16–17, 21, 78, 135, 140, 144, 145–6